THE *NEW* METAL MASTERS

by HP Newquist and Rich Maloof

Backbeat
Books

San Francisco

Published by Backbeat Books
600 Harrison Street, San Francisco, CA 94107
www.backbeatbooks.com
email: books@musicplayer.com

An imprint of CMP Information
Publishers of *Guitar Player*, *Bass Player*, *Keyboard*, and *EQ* magazines

CMP
United Business Media

Distributed to the book trade in the US and Canada by
Publishers Group West, 1700 Fourth Street, Berkeley, CA 94710

Distributed to the music trade in the US and Canada by
Hal Leonard Publishing, P.O. Box 13819, Milwaukee, WI 53213

Cover and text design: Richard Leeds – bigwigdesign.com
Cover photo: ©2004 Rahav Segev/Photopass.com

Library of Congress Cataloging-in-Publication Data

Newquist, H. P. (Harvey P.)
 The new metal masters / by HP Newquist and Rich Maloof.
    p. cm. — (The way they play)
  ISBN 0-87930-804-4 (alk. paper)
 1. Guitar—Instruction and study. 2. Heavy metal (Music)—Instruction
and study. 3. Rock music—Instruction and study. 4. Guitarists—
Biography. I. Maloof, Rich. II. Title. III. Series.

MT580.N48 2004
787.87'166—dc22

                                    2004000545

Printed in the United States of America
04 05 06 07 08   5 4 3 2 1

CONTENTS

INTRODUCTION

Metal of the musical kind has been around in a variety of forms for nearly 40 years. The first metal bands took their inspiration from the minor-key wailing of bluesmen from the American South—and then amplified the hell out of it. These bands were almost all British, many of them from industrial towns far from the London club scene. The sound they made was like nothing else ever heard before. It was as if American blues crossed over the ocean, swallowed a ferocious dose of raw Birmingham steel, and spat back heavy metal.

Purveyed first and foremost by Black Sabbath, with chrome-plated enhancements courtesy of Led Zeppelin and Deep Purple, metal became the definitive musical fusion of electricity, aggression, and anger. Moreso than punk, which was less focused and more chaotic, metal was specifically about conveying pain, alienation, and angst with the sound of hammering guitars, droning bass, and lumbering drums. Metal wasn't even about the lyrics—it was about the way the instruments made you feel. No other music, then or now, captured the feeling of isolation and darkness that is part and parcel of teenage alienation. So pervasive is its pull that metal still has legions of adherents who are many decades out of their teens.

For its first 20 years, metal built on the foundation constructed by Sabbath and its kin. Even the second generation of metal—the New Wave of British Heavy Metal—remained solidly in the doom-and-dirge camp of its forebears. Judas Priest, Iron Maiden, Dio, and their peers added speed and flash, along with harmless satanic images and sword and sorcery, to the lugubrious and mournful underpinnings of early metal. Bands like Whitesnake and Def Leppard added sexual swagger to the sound and propelled metal to the top of the pop charts in the 1980s.

The wild card in this evolution was Motörhead. Lemmy and his band ratcheted up metal's frenzy level and turned down the doom, playing with a feral intensity that even punks had to admire. The musicianship wasn't at the level of guitarists like Sabbath's Tony Iommi or Priest's Glenn Tipton and K.K. Downing or Whitesnake's John Sykes, but that was beside the point. It was only about feel—especially feeling angry.

All of this reached its apex with the success of Metallica and the popularity of Megadeth. A veritable Sabbath on speed, Metallica changed the nature of metal by introducing rhythms that were played in tempos and time signatures more commonly associated with progressive rock and fusion. The demonic imagery was still there, as were the droning bass and plodding drums, but now the guitars were blistering away at piston-pounding speeds. The introduction of a staccato right-hand style transformed metal into something that could actually blister a listener's ears.

With Motörhead, Metallica, and Megadeth, the concept of metal changed dramatically. Nascent metal bands began finding inspiration in a wider variety of musical styles. No longer content to play only blues forms, new metal guitarists were as likely to be influenced by genres ranging from industrial, goth, and grunge to techno, punk, and prog. There was no longer just one form of metal; there were dozens, all heavy in their own right. There was thrash, served up by the defiantly pissed-off Anthrax, Slayer, and Sacred Reich. Rap metal (also called rapcore) was the domain of urban bands like Faith No More, Suicidal Tendencies, and Biohazard. Goth metal from Type-O Negative, Cathedral, and Paradise Lost took the gloom of horror movies, combined it with the surreal dread of bands like the Cure and Sisters of Mercy, and forged it into something decidedly deadly. Ministry and Nine Inch Nails melded drum machines and solid walls of guitar to apocalyptic, party-at-the-end-of-the-world lyrics. Doom metal, notable for its heavily detuned guitars, was played as if its proponents—including Sepultura and My Dying Bride—were playing on the last day of the world. Death metal, considered the seriously evil twin of doom metal, was all about gore and dismembered body parts, as evidenced by bands like Cannibal Corpse, Kreator, and Deicide.

Finally, there was grindcore. A distinctly European form of metal, it harkened back to Sabbath with its slow and bludgeoning riffs. Yet in the hands of Godflesh, Napalm Death, and Carcass, it was also experimental metal. Grindcore incorporated elements of industrial and techno, using layered guitars to replicate the sounds of a world where machines crushed the human spirit on a monstrous assembly line of alienation and hopelessness. It was the sound of Guitarmaggedon.

Of all these metal variations spawned in the underground of the late 1980s and early 1990s, it was the two most unlikely forms—rapcore and grindcore—that would herald the birth of the new metal of the millennium. The mid-1990s saw the popularity of Metallica soar, but hastened the demise of traditional heavy metal even at a time when modern derivatives like Alice in Chains and Soundgarden were enjoying success in the era of grunge. Bands like Judas Priest and Anthrax found themselves without a label, while groups like Def Leppard found themselves without an audience.

But the approaching turn of the century marked a sudden and unexpected shift back to metal, albeit in variegated forms. Tool garnered airplay and critical acclaim with its dark visions and progressive musical approach. A number of rap-influenced, fashion-conscious groups earned the "nu metal" moniker: Korn added lyrics listeners could actually understand to the detuned drone of grindcore and found itself selling millions of albums, and bands like Linkin Park and Limp Bizkit dropped the rage from rapcore and began dominating the charts. Suddenly, a slew of metal groups—from Deftones and Disturbed on to Godsmack and P.O.D.—were benefiting from an interest in all things metal.

That's where metal finds itself in the 21st century. There's more metal, and more metal variations, than ever before. Once given up for dead, metal has mutated like a lethal virus to become the reigning form of rock. New metal is everywhere: the sound-tracks to big-budget action movies, the themes to sporting events, even commercials for sports cars.

This book covers the guitarists who have had the most influence in creating—and propagating—new metal. Some of these players have been around for more than a decade; others are just now emerging. In every case, they've brought something unique to the metal table. Our intention is to offer a clear and complete picture of how these players do what they do best. We're presuming that players who read this book and learn from its examples already have a basic knowledge of the guitar. Because of that, we haven't revisited fundamental lessons or defined terms we think you'll already be familiar with. Instead, we've included biographies, gear, discographies, setups, and characteristic techniques for the artists covered.

The New Metal Masters is the third book in the series The Way They Play. We created The Way They Play so that musicians could explore and experience various guitar styles at a number of different levels, from history and discography to gear setup and lessons. Like our first two books, *The Blues-Rock Masters* and *The Acoustic-Rock Masters*, *The New Metal Masters* immerses guitarists quickly into one of the most popular styles of guitar playing.

Anyone wishing to add new styles and even new tricks to their repertoire will find plenty of material in the pages that follow and on the accompanying CD. It is our hope that we can give guitarists a new perspective on the artists covered and provide you with valuable insight into the way they play.

—*HP Newquist and Rich Maloof*

NOTATIONAL SYMBOLS

The following symbols are used in *The New Metal Masters* to notate fingerings, techniques, and effects commonly used in guitar music. Certain symbols are found in either the tablature or the standard notation only, not both. For clarity, consult both systems.

4 : Left-hand fingering is designated by small Arabic numerals near note heads (1=first finger, 2=middle finger, 3=third finger, 4=little finger, t=thumb).

p : Right-hand fingering designated by letters (p=thumb, i=first finger, m=middle finger, a=third finger, c=little finger).

② : A circled number (1-6) indicates the string on which a note is to be played.

⊓ : Pick downstroke.

V : Pick upstroke.

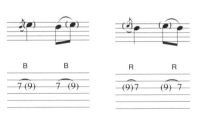

Bend: Play the first note and bend to the pitch of the equivalent fret position shown in parentheses.

Reverse Bend: Prebend the note to the specified pitch/fret position shown in parentheses. Play, then release to indicated pitch/fret.

Hammer-on: From lower to higher note(s). Individual notes may also be hammered.

Pull-off: From higher to lower note(s).

Slide: Play first note and slide up or down to the next pitch. If the notes are tied, pick only the first. If no tie is present, pick both.

A slide symbol before or after a single note indicates a slide to or from an undetermined pitch.

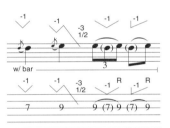

Finger vibrato.   **Bar vibrato.**

Bar dips, dives, and bends: Numerals and fractions indicate distance of bar bends in half-steps.

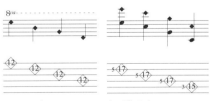

Natural harmonics.   **Artificial harmonics.**

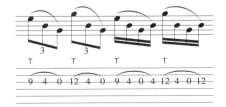

Pick-hand tapping: Notes are hammered with a pick-hand finger, usually followed by additional hammer-ons and pull-offs.

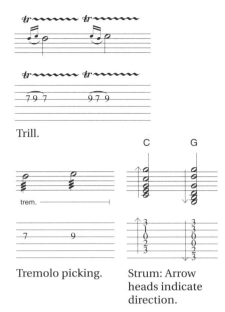

Trill.

Tremolo picking.   **Strum:** Arrow heads indicate direction.

HOW TABLATURE WORKS

The horizontal lines represent the guitar's strings, the top line standing for the high *E*. The numbers designate the frets to be played. For instance, a 2 positioned on the first line would mean play the 2nd fret on the first string (0 indicates an open string). Time values are indicated on the standard notation staff seen directly above the tablature. Special symbols and instructions appear between the standard and tablature staves.

CHORD DIAGRAMS

In all chord diagrams, vertical lines represent the strings, and horizontal lines represent the frets. The following symbols are used:

▬▬▬▬ Nut; indicates first position.

X Muted string, or string not played.

O Open string.

⌒ Barre (partial or full).

● Placement of left-hand fingers.

III Roman numerals indicate the fret at which a chord is located.

Arabic numerals indicate left-hand fingering.

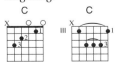

CHAPTER 1
Tool · A Perfect Circle

ADAM JONES OF TOOL

Tool is new metal in the best sense of the term. Beyond that, however, the band defies definition. Art metal, prog metal, even "thinking man's metal" have all been used to try to classify the group—and all fall short. Unlike other new metal masters, many of whom use elements of techno, rap, funk, or hip-hop in their playing, Tool guitarist Adam Jones goes back to the more eclectic and even surreal sounds of bands like King Crimson and Pink Floyd, where complexity, frequent time and rhythmic changes, and a variety of tones are all brought into the mix.

Tool and Jones are enormously influential in modern metal. This is due not only to the uncompromising integrity of Tool's music, but to the musical skills of its members. Contributing to its reputation and its integrity is the fact that the music is everything in Tool. The band members never appear in their videos, their live performances leave them shrouded in stage lights, their pictures do not grace the covers of their albums, and they don't appear on magazine covers. And yet Tool's brand of metal has been mimicked by more new metal bands than any other group since Black Sabbath.

BIOGRAPHY

Tool's singular sound comes from guitarist Jones (born January 15, 1965, in Libertyville, Illinois). He played violin proficiently as a child, but switched to standup bass in high school and played in his school orchestra. In addition, his father owned a guitar and showed Adam the instrument's basic chords. After that, Adam began jamming with his friend Tom Morello (later of Rage Against The Machine). Although Jones was, at the time, the better guitarist, he chose to play bass in the

Jones and one of his silverburst Les Pauls—traditional gear for an unconventional player.

twosome's first band, Electric Sheep. His primary influences were the masters of the progressive and experimental music of the 1970s and '80s, such as Yes's Steve Howe and Crimson's Robert Fripp. He found that textured playing with different sonic elements was more appealing than riffing and soloing—a preference that would later inform Tool's guitar sound.

After graduation, Jones chose to go to art school rather than pursue music. He moved to Los Angeles, where he attended the Hollywood Makeup Academy. His training there got him work in the film industry as a special effects artist, creating designs for the *Predator*, *Jurassic Park*, and *Terminator* film franchises. During this time, he met vocalist Maynard James Keenan through a mutual friend, and the two of them started jamming simply for fun. Keenan lived upstairs from drummer Dan Carey, who would play for the two on those occasions when their regularly scheduled drummer didn't show. The threesome got together regularly, added mutual acquaintance Paul D'Amour on bass, and found that their part-time band was becoming a nearly full-time endeavor.

Hitting the LA clubs, Tool quickly gained a reputation for its dark, almost trance-like excursions into metal. The band fueled its mystique by claiming to be a "tool" for the practice of lachrymology—the science and therapy of crying as outlined in a 1948 book called *A Joyful Guide to Lachrymology*, written by one Ronald Vincent (it took years for fans to figure out that the book and the science were fictional). Although the band members were apparently content in their day jobs—notably Jones, who had a good thing going in the movie business—no one in the group could resist the allure of the music business when Zoo Records offered them a contract in 1991.

Zoo immediately released 1992's *Opiate* EP, a collection of songs that showcased Tool as an emerging "alternative band" as opposed to a grunge band. A year later, Tool put out *Undertow*. In spite of the alt-rock tag, the record revealed Tool's penchant for metallic power chords and feral doses of noise in the framework of longer, less traditional song structures. Songs like "Prison Sex" and "Sober" were punishing doses of multi-textured darkness, filled with thick guitar chords complemented by strange guitar noise.

The band took *Undertow* to the masses by going on tour as part of Lollapalooza. Despite almost no airplay—except on MTV, which creamed itself over Adam Jones's special effects–driven videos—the band's record went platinum. But after the tour, bassist D'Amour left to play guitar in the experimental pop band Lusk. He was replaced by Justin Chancellor, whose band Peach had opened for Tool in Europe. The new lineup went back to the studio but produced no new music. With no comment on future plans from the band, it was if Tool had gone on extended vacation—or ceased to exist.

Undertow held fans over for the three years it took Tool to release the follow-up, 1996's *Ænima*. The world had swung away from grunge and was back in the grips of metal, and Tool was in the right place at the right time. Jones's love for prog rock influenced the group's decision to do long, almost epic-length songs—by metal standards. There were even traces of Middle Eastern melodies in his swirling riffs, along with gently chiming chords ("Pushit") and strange rhythmic changes ("H."). Yet these compositions became staples of underground and all-metal stations, with the six-and-a-half-minute song "Ænema" becoming one of the most popular metal tunes of the late '90s. Riding a huge wave of popularity and critical respect, Tool co-headlined a tour with Korn in 1997—and then disappeared again.

In 2000 Keenan launched a side project, A Perfect Circle, with Jones's guitar tech, Billy Howerdel (see page 15). Rumors of Tool's breakup ran rampant—it had been four years since *Ænima*—but the delay was a result of legal problems with the new ownership of Zoo Records and not creative differences in the band. For a time they held off rumors with the release of *Salival*, a CD/DVD mixed bag of live tracks and unreleased material. When the record company problems were resolved, and with Keenan back from A Perfect Circle, Tool put out *Lateralus*, a stunning album with heightened levels of everything the group was known for. There was the scratched string rasp and gentle picking of "The Grudge," the psychedelic wah-wah of "The Patient," and the out-of-control engine blast of "Parabola." The record debuted at No. 1, proving that Tool could take as long as it wanted to make a record and there would still be a huge audience. There was even a single from the album, "Schism," which highlighted all the elements of Jones's playing, from oddly timed riffs to brutal jackhammer chords and hints of art rock.

As of this writing, the band is on yet another hiatus, and A Perfect Circle has released its second album, *The Thirteenth Step*. In the meantime, metal guitarists will continue to devour and learn from the music that Tool has already created.

GEAR & SETUP

For such a complex player, Jones keeps his equipment choices simple. He plays Gibsons religiously—primarily silverburst Les Paul Customs from the late '70s and early '80s and SGs. He usually sets the guitar to the bridge pickup, leaving the neck pickup in the off position so that he can cut the signal quickly. Tone pots are set either all the way on or all the way off.

He always runs his signal through three amps at a time to get a thick sound comprising different tonal layers: a Marshall bass head, a Sunn Beta Lead (which occasionally gets swapped for a Mesa/Boogie Dual Rectifier), and a Diezel. Jones's effect choices are also fairly basic: a Dunlop 535Q wah-wah pedal, a Boss EQ, and an Ibanez digital delay and flanger.

In the studio, individual songs are usually cut with only one guitar track running through the multiple heads; overdubs are rare. On those occasions when there is more than one layer of guitar, it's usually just Jones doubling to get a fuller sound.

His concert setup mimics his studio setup as he strives to play his live parts so they sound like the album.

STYLE & TECHNIQUE

Adam Jones, like his music, is hard to categorize. He favors big-sounding chords— but they are rarely played in a standard fashion. He will change up frequently, moving from single sustained strums to quick changes that approximate riffs. He admits to writing his parts inside blues scales, although the finished product has little similarity to anything bluesy. This is because he views his compositions cinematically and builds them with different "scenes" requiring different approaches on the guitar.

When he does riff, the lines are simplistic, almost like vocal lines (note "Bottom" from *Undertow* and "Schism" from *Lateralus*). They aren't catchy or even always identifiable as riffs because of their length. And he may fit half a dozen different riffs together in the course of one tune. His solos aren't composed like typical leads, either. They tend to be short, repeated sections within the song and are rarely improvisational in nature. Individual notes are often sustained, fed back, and echoed, giving the sense of a more intricate solo ("Sober" being a prime example). He will also use a small cluster of high notes, often in octave form, for transitioning between song sections.

Like his friend Tom Morello, Jones thrives on coming up with new ways to coax sound out of his guitar. He has admitted to using everything from a lady's shaver and a vibrator to appliance motors to produce strange guitar tones. He holds these devices over the pickups and adjusts the speed with his thumb, eliciting different squawks and squeals from his guitar.

He regularly plays in dropped-*D* tuning, and also uses a drop *B*/*E* combination (6th string *B*, 5th string *E* instead of *A*). He developed the latter to get a more "evil" tone before 7-string guitars became popular in metal.

SELECTED DISCOGRAPHY: TOOL

Opiate EP (Zoo)
Undertow (Zoo)
Aenima (Volcano)
Lateralus (Volcano)

RECOMMENDED CUTS

"Sweat" (*Opiate*)
"Sober" (*Undertow*)
"Prison Sex" (*Undertow*)
"Aenema" (*Aenima*)
"Stinkfist" (*Aenima*)
"Jimmy" (*Aenima*)
"Schism" (*Lateralus*)
"The Grudge" (*Lateralus*)
"Reflection" (*Lateralus*)

BILLY HOWERDEL OF A PERFECT CIRCLE

At first glance, the only connection between A Perfect Circle and Tool is that they share a lead singer. The reality is that A Perfect Circle is the creation of Adam Jones's former guitar tech, Billy Howerdel—a fact that has more to do with A Perfect Circle's sound than Maynard James Keenan's vocals.

Howerdel grew up listening to Randy Rhoads and learning to shred, then fell under the influence of texture guitarists Robert Smith of the Cure and Johnny Marr

SELECTED DISCOGRAPHY: A PERFECT CIRCLE

(both on Virgin)
Mer de Noms
Thirteenth Step

RECOMMENDED CUTS

"Judith" (*Mer de Noms*)
"The Hollow" (*Mer de Noms*)
"Thinking of You" (*Mer de Noms*)

of the Smiths. But Howerdel decided he didn't want to be onstage every night—at least not in front of crowds. Instead, he became a music software expert and guitar tech, signing up with Adam Jones for the tour that followed Tool's debut, *Undertow*. When bassist Paul D'Amour left Tool, Howerdel actually filled in on bass while the *Ænima* album was being written and received a nod on that album's liner notes.

Howerdel also spent time teching for other notables, including Smashing Pumpkins and Guns N' Roses. His most notable gig was getting hired by Trent Reznor as programmer and guitar tech for Nine Inch Nails' *The Downward Spiral* tour. All the while, he kept his own guitar prowess on a back burner and out of sight.

While on various tours, Howerdel had long been in the habit of writing and recording his own songs during his downtime, using his computer to put the songs together. He ultimately thought about turning his songs into a full-fledged studio project, perhaps with a female vocalist. He was sharing a house with Tool's Keenan at the time, and he asked Keenan what he thought about the idea. Keenan's response was that he wanted to do the vocals on Howerdel's project—and turn it into a full band. From there, A Perfect Circle was born.

Once they had worked out Keenan's legal entanglements (he and Tool were at war with their record company), Howerdel added female bassist Paz Lenchantin, second guitarist Troy Van Leeuwen (from Failure), and ace drummer Josh Freese to the fledgling group. Howerdel's "kid in a bedroom" recordings soon became a full-fledged major-label magnet, and the band ultimately signed with Virgin. The first APC record, *Mer de Noms*, was released in 2000 and quickly found itself atop the music charts. While the project had a touch of Tool to it, the playing and instrumentation were not wielded with such a foreboding hand; acoustic guitars and ethereal noises buried deep in the mix gave the record an almost ghostly quality. Howerdel also wrote catchy riffs (notably the first single, "Judith," and "The Hollow"), but that didn't prevent him from indulging in the same kind of sonic eeriness that was Adam Jones's stock-in-trade, using otherworldly effects and guitar sounds to enhance the heavily reverbed crunching of the songs' main themes.

After touring, Keenan went back to Tool and Howerdel went back to writing. Recording was done as time permitted, but the extensive lulls cost the band two members. Lenchantin went to join Billy Corgan's thankfully short-lived Zwan, and

Billy Howerdel—from guitar tech to metal master in 360°.

Van Leeuwen joined a revitalized Queens of the Stone Age. This set off a game of incestuous musical chairs that resulted in Danny Lohner, Nine Inch Nails' touring guitarist, temporarily stepping in to help Howerdel; Corgan's former Pumpkins bandmate Billy Iha joining in Van Leeuwen's place; and former Marilyn Manson bassist Jeordie White (aka Twiggy Ramirez) replacing Paz. Despite the upheaval, the band released its second album, *Thirteenth Step*, in late 2003. If anything, it was even more ornate and lushly orchestrated than its predecessor, yet it still retained the solid underpinnings of *Mer de Noms*.

Howerdel's background as a guitar tech makes him an authority on guitar gear, but he doesn't use much. He plays a Les Paul Classic outfitted with Tom Anderson pickups—and that's his only guitar. To get his crunching tone, he plays through a modified 1978 Marshall Super Lead with a VHT cabinet. For additional effects, he uses a DigiTech 2101 preamp/processor and a Lexicon MPX effects processor. Hard to believe, but that's all it requires to put together A Perfect Circle's guitar sound. In his studio the signal runs to a computer loaded with Pro Tools hardware and Emagic's Logic software.

LESSON

Sliding single notes and power chords establish the motif that holds together this part, characteristic of early Tool (Ex. 1). It may be one or two passes before you decide which fingers to take the slides with, since you can be left out of position to catch the phrases that follow. All the power chords on the open 6th (detuned) and 5th strings are played with downstrokes. A chorus effect thickens the tone and causes it to warble a bit, even making the 3rd-string *B* go a little sour.

Ex. 1: Tool

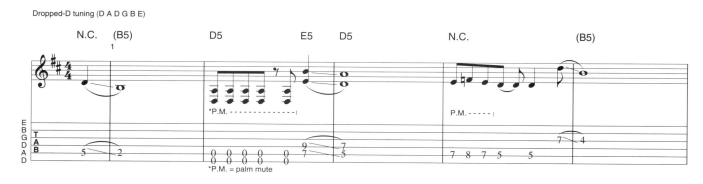

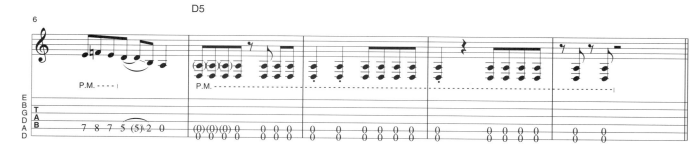

Adam Jones establishes a new take on the heavy-metal gallop with driving parts like the one in Ex. 2, and the feel of this 6/8 groove gains even more momentum when pushed by a drummer. The open dropped-*D* string is used like a pedal against a restless 5th- and 4th-string riff—and again it's *all* downstrokes, even the quick riff. Keep it punchy and taut with palm mutes. Let the bottom string ring at the release into strummed triple-stops.

Ex. 2: Tool

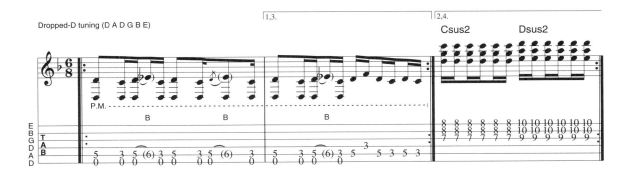

Example 3 is a quick study in contrast, with the middle section differentiated from the surrounding measures by time signature, tone, harmony, and technique.

Start by setting your amp's gain at about halfway and your guitar's volume a bit attenuated; that will give you a relatively clean tone for the opening *B* minor arpeggio in 7/8 time. At bar 5, drive the tone with strong strokes on the power chords. Here the tension breaks not only with the overdrive and by coming off the *B* minor, but with a change to 6/8. Stay on your toes, because you'll need to bring it all back down—and quickly—for a return to the arpeggio in 7/8. Light chorusing again adds a slightly sick off-tune tone.

Ex. 3: Tool

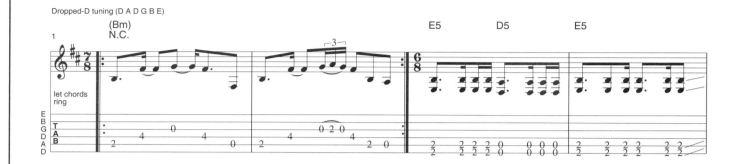

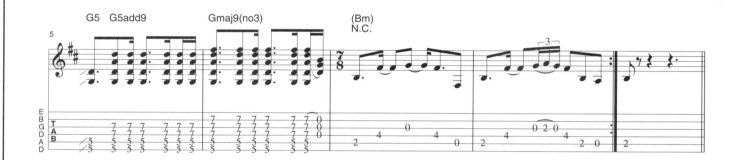

For A Perfect Circle, it takes little more than two complementary guitars in contrary motion to turn the mundane into the epic. In Ex. 4, Guitar 1 chugs on steadily climbing palm mutes (note there's no accent on the first group of 16th-notes) before opening up for the *B* and *E* chords (with guitars detuned a half-step). That's where the octaves of Guitar 2 kick in.

Octave moves like those found in this example are far more typical in jazz than in metal, but Billy Howerdel often uses them to create haunting lines. After the 3rd-and-1st-string octaves, you're down to the 5th-and-3rd-string pairs, which move around quickly for the *C–D–E♭–D* figure in eighth-notes. A dose of digital delay sets Guitar 2's part back in the mix a bit and helps the thinner lines ring and echo over the relatively thick rhythm part.

Ex. 4: A Perfect Circle

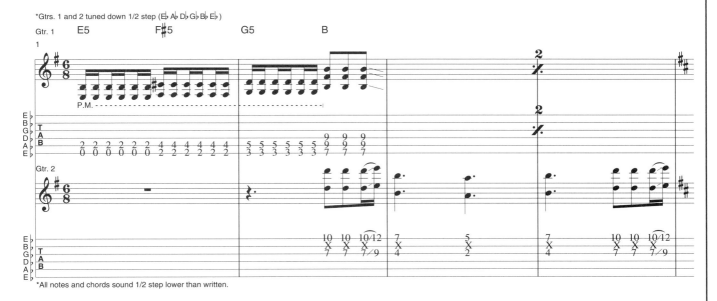

*Gtrs. 1 and 2 tuned down 1/2 step (Eb Ab Db Gb Bb Eb)

*All notes and chords sound 1/2 step lower than written.

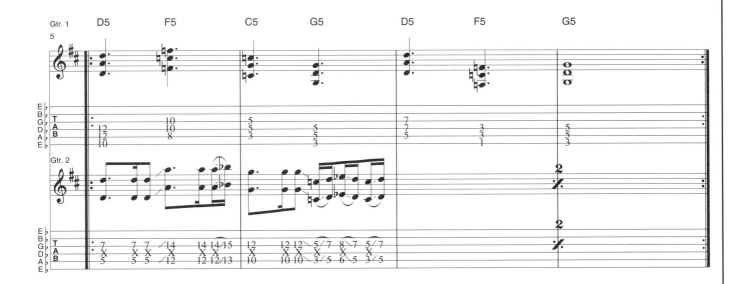

CHAPTER 2
Rage Against The Machine • Audioslave • P.O.D.

TOM MORELLO OF RAGE AGAINST THE MACHINE AND AUDIOSLAVE

Tom Morello's playing in Rage Against The Machine defined the synthesis of street rap and heavy metal. His funky and battering rhythms coupled with sonic experimentation set him apart as an original in an increasingly crowded field of copycats. The conviction of his political beliefs, moreover, established Morello as someone who passionately used the guitar as an extension of himself—and not as a gimmick.

Morello's success in taking what he'd created in Rage and transforming it into Audioslave—new metal's first supergroup—shows how unique and accessible his style really is. From funky rap metal to quirky mainstream metal, Morello has proven to be quite the guitar chameleon, and one who has been at the forefront of new metal for more than a decade.

BIOGRAPHY

Tom Morello may be the most unlikely guitarist to ever play new metal, let alone be considered a leader of the movement. He was born in Harlem, New York, on May 30, 1964, to an unusual duo: Morello's mother was an Irish-Italian free-speech advocate and his father was an African revolutionary who helped liberate Kenya from British rule. At the age of three Morello moved with his mother from New York City to the decidedly whitebread hamlet of Libertyville, Illinois. As the only black kid in town, Morello learned firsthand the ugliness of racism. That experience, in tandem with his mother's activism, led him to develop a strong social conscience and develop an equally strong political stance.

Morello was drawn to the guitar by the playing of Ace Frehley and Jimmy Page. His first attempt at learning the instrument was paying a local guitar player to teach him a Kiss song. But when the teacher insisted on going over the fundamentals first, Morello ditched the idea. Still drawn to the guitar, he heard the Sex Pistols and realized that the guitar could be used as a form of political expression, regardless of the amount of ability—or lack thereof—that the musician possessed. He formed a high school band called Electric Sheep, a name taken from the title of a Philip K. Dick novel and providing evidence of Morello's infatuation with science fiction. (Sci-fi references can be found throughout his work.) The bass player in Electric Sheep was Morello's friend Adam Jones, who would later go on to found one of rock's pre-eminent metal bands, Tool.

After high school Morello's political inclinations led him to Harvard University. Feeling excluded from the upper crust of society that typically attends the university, Morello practiced his guitar several hours each day—and still graduated in 1986 with a degree in social science. Not wanting to pursue life as a lawyer or banker—although he wanted to make waves by working "within the system"—he headed to Los Angeles in an attempt to find fellow musicians who would embrace social change and activism the way that British punks had.

However, he hit LA at the apex of the big-hair metal movement, and few people cared about social change. Plus, Morello's playing was not about shredding solos or sexy, stupid lyrics—it was more about feel and sound. He even kept a noise chart, on which he wrote down settings for strange sounds or noises he stumbled on while experimenting with effects and unusual fingerings. In 1988 Morello formed a group called Lock Up, which signed a one-off deal with the then-fledgling Geffen Records. But their debut album, *Something Bitchin' This Way Comes*, disappeared almost as soon as it was released in 1989. So did the band.

Morello, disgusted with the politics of his record company, quit music and went to work in Senator Alan Cranston's office—figuring that being in an office with a liberal California Democrat might be a better way to get his own voice heard. When Cranston left office a year later, Morello was without a job or a conduit for his politics. While looking for work, he met Zack de la Rocha, a similarly angry young man who had made a local name for himself as a rap freestyler. After listening to what they each could do, the two decided to combine their energies and in 1991 formed Rage Against The Machine. They enlisted Brad Wilk as drummer and Tim Commerford to play bass.

Fusing Morello's love for big rock chords and de la Rocha's pinched rapper's yelp, the band immediately attracted attention for their wild shows. Despite the interest of several major labels, RATM decided to stay independent, believing that the

Tom Morello and his "Arm the Homeless" Strat.

record companies viewed the band's political leanings as only a gimmick. RATM recorded its own EP and sold 5,000 copies, which brought the labels back in a serious way. Signing with Epic, RATM released its self-titled debut in late 1992. The band set out for an extensive tour in support of the record, aligning itself with and supporting major political action organizations. Within a year, the record went platinum and spawned two hits—"Bombtrack" and "Killing in the Name."

The band members' penchant for championing individual leftist causes generated internal friction, and it took four years before Rage was able to complete and release its sophomore effort, *Evil Empire*. Pent-up demand sent the record to No. 1 upon its release in 1996. The disc featured "Bulls on Parade," a hugely explosive tune with a riff vaguely reminiscent of Led Zeppelin's "Immigrant Song." Morello's playing evolved into a style that incorporated bizarre sound effects and noise toys—much like a funk version of former David Bowie sidekick Reeves Gabrels.

RATM toured with Wu-Tang Clan and showed up to play high-profile benefit concerts around the U.S. In 1999, RATM released *The Battle of Los Angeles*, which—like its predecessor—debuted at No. 1. Their visibility was heightened even further by the inclusion of "Wake Up" (from their first album) as the nominal theme song to *The Matrix*.

Despite the successful run, the following year de la Rocha abruptly announced that he was leaving the band to pursue a solo career. Shocked, the remaining members released *Renegades*, an album of tunes previously recorded with de la Rocha. It proved to be RATM's final record.

Down but not out, Morello, Wilk, and Commerford stayed together and found an unlikely replacement for de la Rocha—Soundgarden's Chris Cornell. After the dissolution of Soundgarden, Cornell had gotten a tepid response to his solo record, *Euphoria Morning*, in 1999. Brought together by Rick Rubin, the project aimed to fuse the best of Rage's rap metal and Soundgarden's psychedelic grunge metal. The four recorded together, but the results were held up and nearly derailed by the band's various managers. The four members worked their way out of the jam by hiring a third-party management firm to represent the entire group, and Audioslave was born.

Billed as the first alternative rock/metal supergroup, Audioslave hit the ground running in November 2002. The popularity of the respective members propelled the band's eponymous debut to the top of the charts in the summer of 2003. Surprisingly, Morello's playing was more heavy rock and less funk than it had been in his previous bands. Part of this was due to Cornell's songwriting, which emphasized a grittier melody-driven sound without any rapped lyrics. (Cornell also refused to write anything politically charged.) Morello was now playing with a singer who actually sang instead of shouting lyrics out in cadence. Plus, Cornell could handle a guitar, and many of his compositions featured the interplay of his and Morello's parts.

Morello, meanwhile, gave free rein to his experimental side, as if he were finally more interested in the guitar than in politics. Several of Audioslave's cuts, notably "Shadow on the Sun" and "Like a Stone," featured Morello stretching his boundaries as a soloist and displaying an affinity for the blues. His effects use went into overdrive as well, sounding as if he had dug deep into Steve Vai's bag of aural tricks with whooping trills, harmonized echoes, and whammy-bar divebombs.

The success of both Audioslave and Rage was dependent on Morello's ability to deliver truly interesting and compelling guitar parts that complemented dynamic lead singers. His ability to do that—and still make room for invention and experimentation—will serve Morello well in the annals of metal and in music yet to come.

GEAR & SETUP

Morello has used Fenders—both Telecasters and Strats—for much of his career, along with a variety of Ibanez models. Perhaps his most notable guitar, though, is one known simply as "Arm the Homeless." (The words are written on the body.) It started out as a Strat-style custom-made guitar, but Morello has swapped out every piece to the point where only the body remains of the original. He employs a variety of tunings, including dropped-*D* (as in "Renegades of Funk"), and a dropped-*A*, in which the 6th string is tuned one octave lower than the 5th. This requires a gauge of at least .062, and preferably heavier.

Morello has long used Marshall amps, employing a JCM800 2205 50-watt head. His primary cabinets are 4x10 Peaveys. He also occasionally uses a Music Man Twin and a Line 6 Flextone.

Though he is a veteran effects geek, his pedals are fairly mundane. He uses a Boss digital delay and tremolo, a DigiTech Whammy pedal, a DOD FX40B equalizer and delay, an MXR Phase 100, a Vox Tone Bender, and a Dunlop Crybaby wah. Most of these pedals do double duty in the studio and in concert.

STYLE & TECHNIQUE

Morello admits to having gotten involved with the guitar for the sound of it. He claims his biggest influence is a man named Joe Hill, a Swedish immigrant and folksinger who lived in Utah in the early 1900s. Hill was best known, though, as a union organizer and protest leader. No recordings of Joe exist, but Morello liked what Joe stood for.

His first guitar-playing influences were the Sex Pistols and MC5 (although he had long been a fan of bands like Kiss, Led Zeppelin, and Black Sabbath). The Pistols and MC5 played music that was simple, direct, and socially charged. High school friend Adam Jones (later of Tool) taught Morello a lot on the guitar, even though Adam was the bass player in their band.

SELECTED DISCOGRAPHY: TOM MORELLO

with Lock Up
Something Bitchin' This Way Comes (Manifesto)
with Rage Against the Machine
Rage Against the Machine (Epic)
Evil Empire (Epic)
Battle of Los Angeles (Epic)
Renegades (Epic)
with Audioslave
Audioslave (Epic)

RECOMMENDED CUTS
"Wake Up" (*Rage Against the Machine*)
"No Shelter" (*Godzilla* soundtrack)
"Bulls on Parade" (*Evil Empire*)
"Renegades of Funk" (*Renegades*)
"Killing in the Name" (*Rage Against the Machine*)
"Bombtrack" (*Rage Against the Machine*)
"Like a Stone" (*Audioslave*)

When Morello actually started learning the fundamentals and practicing them, he dove in head first, practicing up to eight hours a day while he was in college. He learned all the appropriate shred routines, à la Randy Rhoads, but decided the style didn't really represent him. He was more interested in evoking unlikely sounds from the guitar. To that end, he began playing with his toggle switch, bouncing back and forth between tones and messing with volume settings.

His strength resides in writing riffs that translate well to bombast, especially when coupled with the right drum sound (something he admired in Jimmy Page). They are usually a little long to be hummable riffs, often stretching over several bars, but they are always rooted in a uniquely heavy groove of funk guitar patterns.

His work in Rage was almost minimalist, since it was important that the guitar didn't obscure the politics of the lyrics. As such, his guitar often introduces a song with a big riff, and then heads to the backseat. Many tunes rely on a bass riff to counter the lyric, so Morello can often be found just throwing in quick bursts of guitar fills at the end of a line.

Until Audioslave, his lead playing was more a showcase for sound effects than actual lines—as exemplified by the wah-wah bleating of "No Shelter," the talkbox cadence of "Wake Up," and the yellowjacket droning of "Renegades of Funk." In fact, many of Morello's solos follow a similar pattern—they are simple, monochromatic steps within a scale that are effected in different ways depending on the setting.

Playing off Chris Cornell obviously encouraged Morello to stretch out (since he was still playing with the same rhythm section). While he still relied heavily on his herky-jerky, stutter-stepped lead style for songs such as "Cochise," "Exploder," and "Show Me How to Live"—moving in tiny ascending and descending increments up and down the scale—he did show a lyrical side on the bluesy "Getaway Car" and "The Last Remaining Light."

Audioslave's "Hypnotize" may be the quintessential Morello track. Featuring a droning, siren guitar along with plenty of stuttering sci-fi sound effects, Morello combines heavy riffs and simple chords with punctuated phrases and transitional phrases that accentuate the track and support the vocals.

Audioslave's overall sound owes a lot to Cornell, whose years fronting Soundgarden established his reputation as a rock powerhouse. Cornell and guitarist Kim Thayil created a thick, grungy form of heavy rock that relied more on metal underpinnings than did the music of Seattle compatriots Nirvana and Pearl Jam. Thayil's riffs were often crushing and dark in the vein of Black Sabbath, although the band managed to add a dose of alternative psychedelia to the mix, establishing a unique and accomplished sound that set them apart from and above the rest of the grunge movement.

Marcos Curiel of P.O.D. with his PRS hollowbody; he more typically played a solidbody PRS Custom 22.

MARCOS CURIEL AND JASON TRUBY OF P.O.D.

The band that picked up the discarded mantle of RATM was P.O.D. It mixes heavy metal riffs with the kind of philosophical lyrics that underscored Rage—except in P.O.D. the lyrics are about Christianity, not politics.

Almost militantly Christian, the band wears its religion on its sleeve. Its name is an acronym for Payable on Death, a term that highlights the concept that how you live on Earth determines where you live after you die.

SELECTED DISCOGRAPHY: P.O.D.

Snuff the Punk EP (Butterfly)

Brown (Butterfly)

Live (Diamante Music)

The Warriors EP (Tooth & Nail)

The Fundamental Elements of Southtown (Atlantic)

Satellite (Atlantic)

Payable on Death (Atlantic)

RECOMMENDED CUTS

"Satellite" (*Satellite*)

"Alive" (*Satellite*)

"Southtown" (*The Fundamental Elements of Southtown*)

"Rock the Party (Off the Hook)" (*The Fundamental Elements of Southtown*)

"Portrait" (*Satellite*)

The band was formed in 1992 in San Ysidro, California, by vocalist Paul "Sonny" Sandoval and his cousin, drummer Noah "Wuv" Bernardos. They recruited guitarist Marcos Curiel and bassist Mark "Traa" Daniels to create P.O.D. Curiel grew up in a Hispanic neighborhood near San Diego, where his grandfather was a mariachi player. Curiel's first influence was Carlos Santana, in part because Santana had come from nearby Tijuana. Later he listened to a variety of heavier bands, from Iron Maiden to Jane's Addiction.

Combining hip-hop, jazz, punk, funk, reggae, rap, and metal—with decidedly religious lyrics—the band created a sound that defied description, yet drew comparisons to Bad Brains, RATM, and even Korn.

For most of its career, P.O.D. toured back and forth across the U.S., opening for Green Day and Bad Brains, selling its homemade EPs at shows and garnering a rabid following. After six years on the road and respectable sales of its recordings, the band was signed by Atlantic Records in 1998. P.O.D.'s first album, *The Fundamental Elements of Southtown* (the title refers to San Ysidro's nickname), was released in 1999, and while not quite a breakthrough still sold over a million copies. The band signed on for several metal tours such as Ozzfest and, like all smart metal bands, began feeding its music to Hollywood for use on soundtracks. Ultimately, its songs were featured on *Any Given Sunday*, *Little Nicky*, *The Scorpion King*, and *Blair Witch 2*.

The band hit the big time in 2001 with *Satellite*, an album that featured stunning tunes and radio and MTV staples such as the title track, "Alive," and "Youth of the Nation." With the disbanding of RATM, P.O.D. was the undisputed heavyweight in the rap metal category—religion or no religion. The band was called an overnight success, although it had been nearly 12 years in the making.

Despite the success, all was not well internally. Marcos started chafing at the huge amount of hype that accompanied the band's religious beliefs. He started a side project called Accident Experiment (AX), which—according to him—didn't fit in with the Bible-thumping image that P.O.D. had created for itself and its members. He exited P.O.D., and the band claims he left because he wanted to try something new.

Jason Truby contributing to P.O.D.'s distinctive vocal harmonies.

The real answer may have been in who the band got to replace Marcos. In the summer of 2003, Jason Truby of Living Sacrifice was hired to fill the guitar spot. Living Sacrifice had opened for P.O.D. on a number of occasions, and, like P.O.D., was openly and loudly Christian in its music and attitude.

Truby joined the band in time to help write the main theme for *The Matrix Reloaded*, "Sleeping Awake," and then worked on the band's self-titled third album. A former guitar teacher, Truby was well versed in a variety of styles, notably jazz, and he prompted the band to expand beyond its rap and rock sound. The result was a more polished record with less punk abandon than past efforts, one that—while still heavy—showed a move away from its distinctive rap-oriented sound.

Both players created large snarling tones during their time in P.O.D. Curiel was a huge Paul Reed Smith fan because of the manufacturer's longtime association with

Santana. Curiel favored a PRS Custom 22 equipped with Dragon II pickups and DR strings. For the occasional acoustic piece he used Alvarez guitars. His amps were primarily Mesa/Boogie Triple Rectifiers, although he also used Soldanos, Marshalls, and occasionally a Vox AC30. His effects mirrored those of other nu-metallists: DigiTech Whammy pedal; Boss delay, chorus, flanger, and reverb pedals; MXR Phase 90; Dunlop Univibe chorus and Crybaby wah; and an EBow sustainer. He tuned down a step (*DGCFAD* low to high), and often dropped the lowest *D* to *C*.

Truby's gear is also very standard metal issue. He uses a Gibson Les Paul with SIT strings, and runs it through Mesa/Boogie Double and Triple Rectifiers, a Mesa/Boogie F100, or a Line 6. His effects include a Dunlop Rotovibe, MXR Phase 90, and DigiTech delay. He also employs a Bradshaw switching system.

LESSON

Tom Morello seems to be caught in a weird hyperspace somewhere between Black Sabbath and Parliament/Funkadelic, as Ex. 5's riff bears out. A wah-wah pedal stays on throughout the example. Play the opening single-note line with the wah about three-quarters of the way off the floor for a midrangey and out-of-phase tone.

At bar 5 begin rocking the wah steadily up and down in an even-eighth-note rhythm. Your right-hand strums are likewise steady, alternating between octave *G*'s and choked strings. *Note that the tempo track for this example plays eighth-notes rather than quarters.*

Ex. 5: Rage Against The Machine

Track 5

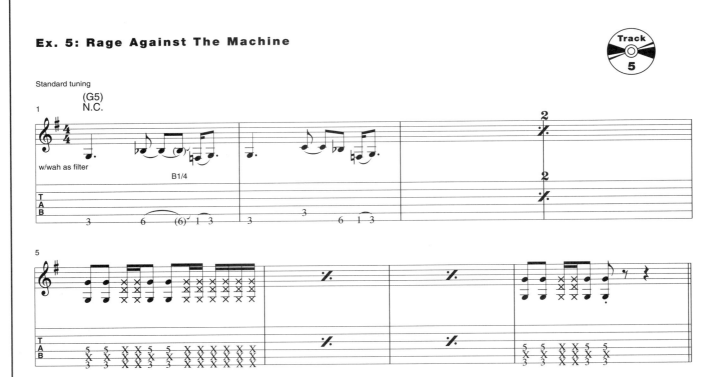

Riff-based Audioslave tunes like "Cochise" and "Set It Off" represent the shared tastes of Tom Morello and Chris Cornell, marking the crossover point where Rage Against The Machine meets Soundgarden. Check the lumbering, slow groove in Ex. 6, where two parts are conjoined in a riff not unlike the Beatles' "Come Together." Both parts are played very clean—no slides into or fall-offs from any note.

Though the two parts play the same notes by name, they alternate in the first part of the phrase between unisons and octaves, which makes for a distinct spread.

Ex. 6: Audioslave

Come solo time, Morello routinely gets quirky. The part in Ex. 7 has been written for the heavy riff in the previous example, but Morello is just as likely to drop a solo like this into a ballad.

It's almost impossible to recreate this kind of line without the aid of a DigiTech Whammy. Set the pedal to "Octave ^" so that depressing the pedal boosts your signal by one octave. For the spacey cries at the top of the solo, anticipate each note (strike the strings just ahead of the beat) with the pedal full up, raking the strings as the pedal is depressed—this gives a giant upward scoop. Try to catch a little downward Whammy effect (pedal back up) after you reach pitch, and add some finger vibrato.

The second half of the solo, at bar 6, is played with the Whammy fully depressed (up a full octave) until the stacked *F♯*s, which get treated with more scoops courtesy of the Whammy.

Ex. 7: Audioslave

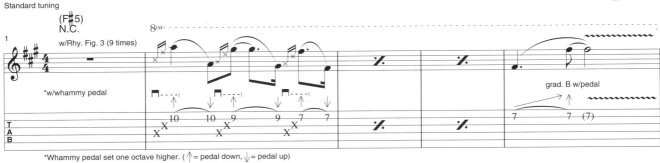

Editing tracks in the studio, producers can easily trim the start and stop times of any given part. So to recreate such parts in the real world, you need to pay extra attention to technique. The clipped feel between phrases in Ex. 8 is purely the result of manual muting. There's also some sleight of hand—or sleight of *foot*—at work. A DigiTech Whammy is set to add a 5th above (shown in parentheses) the note played. Note, however, that the Whammy is quickly stomped off for the fill at the end of bar 4, then back on for the riff's return.

Ex. 8: P.O.D.

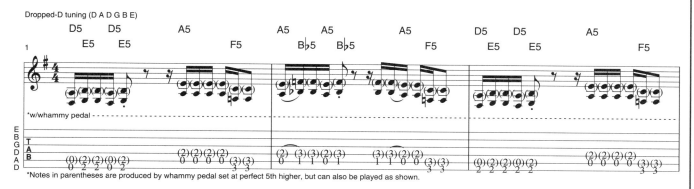

*Notes in parentheses are produced by whammy pedal set at perfect 5th higher, but can also be played as shown.

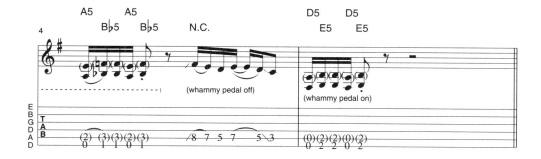

The opening pedal-chord figure in Ex. 9 sounds like it descended from the mighty King's X. Chugging power chords, made easy by the dropped-*D* tuning, play against double-stops starting high on the neck. The trick here is to palm-mute the low power chords but let the higher-voiced double-stops ring. Adding compression helps bring the two parts to competitive volume levels. The chord changes descend, landing on a part that features a new pedal-point, the open *A* string.

Ex. 9: P.O.D.

Track
9

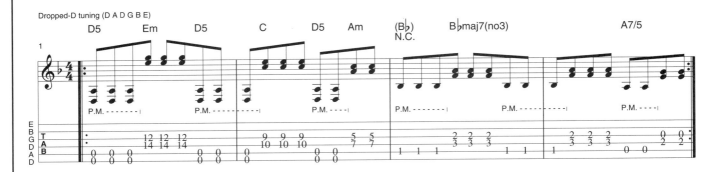

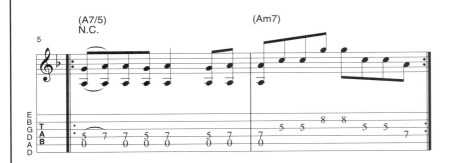

CHAPTER 3
Godflesh · Carcass

JUSTIN BROADRICK OF GODFLESH

When Godflesh released its first album in 1988, there had never been anything before it that sounded so ominous and malevolent. Godflesh was the brainchild of guitarist and occasional vocalist Justin Broadrick, whose goal was to convey sonic emotions of loss, pain, despair, and cruelty—the trademarks of good heavy metal—with a guitar. In that way, he had the same goals as singer-songwriters who used acoustic guitars to create ballads of love and beauty. But Broadrick was headed someplace altogether darker.

Godflesh's severely detuned guitars and slabs of sludge dramatically changed the notion of metal. Forsaking neatly packaged riffs and vocals in favor of subterranean tone, trance-like drones, and clinically precise beat-driven chording, Broadrick bulldozed over the metal of previous generations with startling determination. In his desire to create something that was everything popular music was not, Broadrick took the guitar to places it had never been, paving the way for a new generation of guitarists who would attempt to push the sonic limits of the instrument in every way imaginable.

BIOGRAPHY

Born in Birmingham, England, in 1970, Broadrick encountered the guitar at an early age: His natural father was a bassist and guitarist, while his stepfather was a Pink Floyd/Hendrix enthusiast who kept a Strat around the house. Broadrick started playing the guitar when he was 10, with his stepfather teaching him the basics.

He started with punk music, figuring that any kid with a guitar who knew three chords could be in a punk band. His first musical inspiration was Stranglers guitarist

Hugh Cornwell. Cornwell and the Stranglers were almost avant-punk; their music was simple and direct, yet the guitar and bass played different lines, creating multiple layers in each song. Broadrick heard the dissonance between the two instruments and was drawn to its sound and effect.

Having embraced the Stranglers and their punk ethic, Broadrick found his way to heavier bands like Black Sabbath and Killing Joke. At the age of only 16, Broadrick helped create the first lineup of Napalm Death—the hugely influential band that sowed the seeds of grindcore and doom metal. Broadrick worked on the band's 1987 debut LP, *Scum*, but left before it was completed because he was bored. Wanting to explore other avenues as a musician, he teamed up with the little-known Head of David—as their drummer. Yet his time with HOD was also short-lived as the band started leaning in a commercial metal direction, the antithesis of what Broadrick was looking to do.

In 1988 Broadrick formed Godflesh. He drew his inspiration from German industrial bands like Einstürzende Neubauten that were experimenting with tape noise, electronics, and drum machines. Broadrick's revelation was to use guitars and bass instead of synths and noisemakers to create hypnotic nightmarish sounds. Also drawing from techno and its club orientation, he put dissonant and droning guitars into his mixes to create a trancelike element to his compositions.

In its first incarnation, Godflesh was Broadrick, bassist Ben G.C. Green, and an Alesis drum machine. Outside of an occasional garbled vocal line, Godflesh spurned singing: Broadrick thought the essence of pop music was its vocal lines, and he wanted to be as far removed from pop as he could get.

Although its hallucinogenic and monochromatic sound was based on the clashing of guitars, the music was not just noise and feedback à la Lou Reed's hideously stupid *Metal Machine Music* or Neil Young's extended tinnitus-inducing noodlings on *Weld*. Instead, it was clinically calculated and crafted to make listeners feel one of two emotions: pain or despair—sometimes both. Broadrick called it sad music. Yet it had rhythm, it had sections that could be identified as parts A, B, and C (like verses and choruses), and it had repeating themes that were strangely compelling. Stranger still, people could dance to Godflesh's musical mayhem if so inclined.

Godflesh attracted instant attention for the originality of its sound as well as its stripped-down format. Working digitally, the band released the *Godflesh* EP and a slew of remixes that found their way into London's underground clubs (a practice that continued during its entire lifespan). The band signed with metal label Earache, which put out Godflesh's full-length debut, *Streetcleaner*, in 1989. Listeners were awed. Never before had one band incorporated metal, industrial,

Justin Broadrick and Benny George Christian Green of Godflesh.

techno, and electronica into a single form—let alone one that was so sinister sounding.

Like their club counterparts, Godflesh started releasing EPs and then full-length records every two years. *Streetcleaner* was followed by 1990's *Slavestate* and 1992's *Pure*. Along the way, Broadrick and Green occasionally added other guitarists (Steve Hough, Robert Hampson, Paul Neville) and even a human drummer (notably Ted Parsons from Prong and Brian "Brain" Mantia of Primus). They flirted with ever more extreme doom-laden techno-style dance rhythms, samples, MIDI, and more intense walls of sound, never once forsaking the apocalyptic power of the guitar.

The very thing that defined Godflesh and made them so innovative kept them from gaining widespread appeal. The murderous hammering of guitars and drum machines was perfect for vicious live shows and underground clubs in Europe, but mainstream audiences didn't get it. The lack of real vocals made Godflesh inaccessible except to hardcore listeners and guitarists. Despite Metallica's Kirk Hammett calling them his favorite band, and similar praise for Broadrick from Joe Satriani, Godflesh's brand of Guitarmageddon did not catch on in the U.S.

When Earache was absorbed into Sony, Broadrick and company found themselves on a very major label. Sony released the *Merciless* EP and the *Selfless* album to critical acclaim in 1995, but the band still could not transcend its cult status. Instead, other doom-and-gloom bands, including Nine Inch Nails and Ministry, were creating more radio- and MTV-friendly versions of mechanical-sounding industrial metal. In the process, those bands leapt to the front of the new metal pack.

Complicating matters further was the fact that Godflesh was not Broadrick's only pursuit. In his spare time, if it can be called that, he started two independent record labels, produced several albums, guested on a number of British techno and trance projects, released albums under the names Techno Animal and Ice, and was in huge demand as a remixer (including a production of Pantera's "Walk"). Still, he made the time to put together a full-length Godflesh album every two years, notably *Us and Them* in 1999 and *Hymns* in 2001. But, citing brain drain from his numerous projects and busy touring schedule, Broadrick broke up Godflesh in 2002. Far from retirement, he is currently in the process of developing his next musical venture, Jesu.

Broadrick's Godflesh legacy is one of having steered metal far from its blues roots and toward more experimental forms of music, notably industrial. Bands like Korn have appropriated the dissonance and doom of Godflesh, added accessible vocals and lyrics, and become the popular face of new metal. Yet, when assessing the detuned and dissonant style of most new metal guitarists, it's important to note that Broadrick invented it.

GEAR & SETUP

For someone who is credited with creating some of the heaviest tones in the history of metal, Broadrick chooses gear that is decidedly low-tech. He plays a custom-made Fender Strat with light-gauge strings (and occasionally an Ibanez). Broadrick tunes the entire instrument (and the accompanying bass guitar) down a step and a half to *C#* to maximize the bottom end, and he uses a metal pick to rip high-pitched squeals from the strings.

His amp is an old Marshall JCM800, which he likes because it has high and low inputs—although he only uses the high input. He runs it through a Marshall 4x10 cabinet.

For effects Broadrick employs a Boss digital delay and a Boss Heavy Metal pedal. The delay is set with a sharp slapback to isolate the individual guitars in the mix. He sets the low and high EQs so that they face each other: low is ¾ up, high is ¾ down. There is no midrange at all in Godflesh's music; the tones are set to accentuate highs and lows.

As for recording, Broadrick believes that digital recording equipment is the most accurate way to capture the sound of the guitar as he hears it through his Marshall cabinet. When producing a record, Broadrick wants the Marshall to sound like it's sitting in the listener's room (he remembered "feeling heat" from the stereo speakers when he would listen to his father's albums, and he wanted to make that happen with his records).

STYLE & TECHNIQUE

When the first Godflesh album was released, there was nothing on Earth that sounded like its layers of guitars. Glenn Branca's experimentalism—which featured members of Sonic Youth and Helmet's Page Hamilton—came close, but it wasn't nearly as horrific. Godflesh was the sound of bulldozers on crack, jackhammers as surgical supplies, and sharpened chainsaws as children's toys.

His playing is extraordinarily simple. Chord patterns are repeated, usually with a very heavy-handed strum or strong picking. Droning notes are created with feedback, changing perhaps only once every several bars. Rarely is anything played fast. Speed is actually implied as gain level increases during individual songs, but it rarely gets much faster than a slow-to-moderate dirge.

Broadrick claims little knowledge of theory. Instead, his technique is all about finding dissonance in competing chords, or even within the same chord. He mixes heavy tritone chords seamlessly with hallucinogenic-sounding samples. Repeated listenings usually uncover different guitars following different paths, each as entrancing as the next. He also believes in using the guitar for every part of a track: rhythm, bits of noise, background sounds, and foreground notes. This approach requires him to pay close attention to the tone of each guitar, and how they are all eventually mixed together. His guitar parts are not always distinguishable as guitars—instead, they may sound like air-raid sirens, hydraulic presses, bird screeches, and the sound of locomotives having sex.

SELECTED DISCOGRAPHY: GODFLESH

Godflesh EP (Earache)

Streetcleaner (Earache)

Pure (Earache)

Merciless EP (Sony)

Selfless (Sony)

Songs of Love and Hate (Earache)

Us and Them (Earache)

Hymns (Koch)

Messiah (Relapse)

RECOMMENDED CUTS

"Like Rats" (*Streetcleaner*)

"Wound" (*Streetcleaner*)

"I Wasn't Born to Follow" (*Pure*)

"Blind" (*Merciless*)

"Flowers" (*Merciless*)

"Anything Is Mine" (*Selfless*)

"Angel Domain" (*Songs of Love and Hate*)

"Animals" (*Hymns*)

BILL STEER OF CARCASS

When Justin Broadrick left Napalm Death to pursue his own muse—and ultimately form Godflesh—he was replaced by guitarist Bill Steer. This change came just as Napalm Death's first album, *Scum*, was in the final stages of production. The result was that Broadrick and Steer are featured on different sides of the same record. In later years it was more than a little coincidental that Broadrick's playing would define the detuned and desolate corner of metal in the '90s, while Steer's playing epitomized the speed and frenzy of finger-blistering and -bleeding metal.

Steer got his start in 1985 as a founder of England's Carcass. That band was known for its medically precise and anatomically graphic lyrics and rip-your-flesh brand of metal—a style that spawned the metal of a thousand names: death metal, black metal, gore metal, deathcore, grindcore, gorecore, and even thrash.

While Carcass was struggling to make a name for itself, Napalm Death was making waves and winning raves from John Peel, who had long hosted an influential new music program on the BBC. As Napalm Death prepared to release its first record—complete with songs that lasted only a few seconds—guitarist Justin Broadrick decided to strike out on his own. Steer was asked to help finish the record, and then invited to join the band in Broadrick's stead. He agreed to work part-time for Napalm Death, while still working with Carcass. In 1989, after two years of getting pulled in two musical directions, Steer opted to return full-time to Carcass.

Carcass established its reputation by becoming a metal band like no other. In addition to its gargled-glass vocals and leadpipe riffs, the band incorporated sizzling solos and lead playing that would have been right at home on any shred record of the time—something that was anathema to the lugubrious rhythmic pace of most grindcore bands. In fact, Steer's influences were technical masters like Allan Holdsworth and Yngwie Malmsteen, although Steer's playing was 'roid rage compared to Yngwie's more refined style.

Unlike his metal peers, Steer had no compunction about speeding his way through neo-classical post-Yngwie solos, admirably shredding through the rhythmic

SELECTED DISCOGRAPHY: CARCASS

(all on Earache)
*Necroticism: Descanting the
   Insalubrious*
Tools of the Trade
Heartwork
Swansong

RECOMMENDED CUTS

"Buried Dreams" (*Heartwork*)
"This Mortal Coil" (*Heartwork*)
"Blind Bleeding the Blind" (*Heartwork*)
"Room 101" (*Swansong*)
"R**k the Vote" (*Swansong*)

Shredding metal to death—Bill Steer.

carnage dished out by his bandmates. His melodic and tasteful soloing, which was a huge part of the Carcass sound, pushed the envelope of the traditionally rhythm-shackled new-metal genre. And his assault-rifle riffs were delivered at a speed that could have made James Hetfield gasp for air. Not only were his guitar parts played fast and razor sharp, but as examples of metal they were archetypes of well-honed and speedy chops.

Carcass's early albums, notably *Reek of Putrefaction* and *Necroticism: Descanting the Insalubrious*, were violent servings of metal that were intent on pummeling listeners as much as the instruments. *Heartwork* (1994) was considered the band's breakthrough, and it was a stunning example of what Steer could cook up. Yet, like Justin Broadrick's Godflesh, Carcass couldn't win over American audiences. That chore was left to bands with more radio-savvy chops, and Columbia Records (which had entered into a licensing deal with metal label Earache) was demanding something more radio-friendly from Carcass. As far as Steer was concerned, that wasn't going to happen, so in 1996 Carcass delivered more of the same with *Swansong*. Then Steer abandoned the band, leaving nothing but, well, a carcass—one which more than a few nu-metallers have been happy to feed off in the intervening years.

To get his bone-crushing sound, Steer detuned 2½ steps, to *B*, and used string gauges of .012 to .056. His main guitar was an Ibanez FGM; his amps were Peavey 5150s and Marshalls. In the studio he mixed in a Marshall 10-watt Valvestate for a high-end layer.

LESSON

Many metal players avoid playing dissonant chords when their guitars are heavily distorted, since the notes, and some power, tend to get lost. But Justin Broadrick is fearless. His Strat's single-coil pickups help bring out individual voices as in the chord at the top of Ex. 10's bar 5. Be sure to let the open 3rd string ring in bars 6 and 8 to get the most out of the discordant arpeggio.

Ex. 10: Godflesh

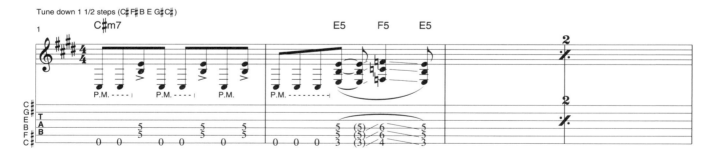

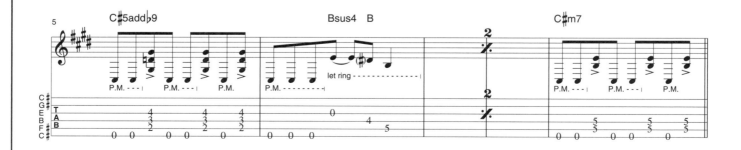

The Marshall JCM800 has an especially brash overdrive, and Broadrick gets the most out of its oppressive crunch. As we've known since Black Sabbath, simple equals heavy, and Ex. 11's straight ride down the neck proves the rule. Don't get lazy, though: the chugging 5 chords in bars 2 and 4 require fast and well-timed downstrokes—*all* downstrokes. Note that on our play-along CD, the *A* note (3rd string, 5th fret in this example, detuned 1½ steps) is doubled.

Ex. 11: Godflesh

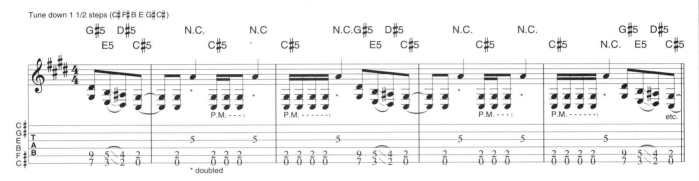

While other metal masters drudged their way through riffs, Bill Steer was flying around the neck and often blurring the line between riffs and leads. Example 12 shows a Carcass-style riff at a reasonable tempo, though galloping notes and quick pull-off figures hint at lightning licks to come. Watch for the early position change: you start in III but are quickly forced into V to catch the *D* at the 8th fret. (Note how far we're detuned.) Then it's back down to II for the palm-muted figures and pinch harmonics that wrap the phrase.

Ex. 12: Carcass

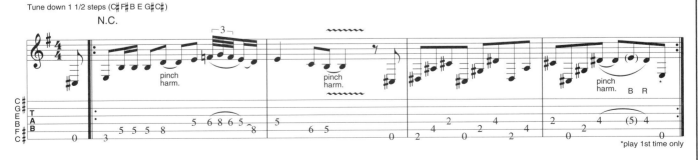

CHAPTER 4
Nine Inch Nails

TRENT REZNOR

Trent Reznor, the one-man band shrink-wrapped within the confines of Nine Inch Nails, merged metal guitars with goth, industrial, and techno to create the definitive sound of new-generation metal. He played guitars and sampled them, splicing and rearranging them in a computerized version of a Cuisinart. In the process, he single-handedly became the transition between the synth- and sample-driven industrial electronica world and the guitar-laden metal world.

Reznor and the way he approached the sound of his guitars—as instruments, as noisemakers, as weapons—revolutionized the way guitars are used in recording. His hugely successful albums contain possibly the most bizarre and intriguing recordings of the instrument ever laid down.

BIOGRAPHY

Born May 17, 1965, in Mercer, Pennsylvania, Reznor was a typically disaffected teenager who turned to music as a release for everything that angered him. Trained as a pianist and a saxophonist—he was a big fan of David Bowie and Brian Eno—he played in the school marching band as well as local rock bands. He also taught himself enough guitar to manage a few chords and play a few songs. As a college student, he pursued computer programming, learning about MIDI, keyboard programming, and sampling to help him create the music he wanted to put down. He moved to Cleveland, where he was given access to a studio in exchange for doing engineering and janitorial work. He also played in a synth-pop band called Exotic Birds and got himself a cameo in the Michael J. Fox/Joan Jett flick *Light of Day*.

With his studio time, he created the outline for an entire album on his own, using the name Nine Inch Nails (which he thought sounded cooler than "Trent Reznor"). He shopped the demo, but the only interest came from TVT Records (then TeeVee Toons), a label built almost entirely on putting together CD packages of TV theme songs. But Reznor went for it, and in 1989 he assembled his first record, *Pretty Hate Machine*. With its lurid underpinnings of alienation, hate, and sex, the album appealed to listeners in a variety of genres, from goth to industrial and metal. The album, which seemed to come from out of nowhere given that it was on a novelty label, sold more than a million copies.

Yet Reznor didn't make any money from *Pretty Hate Machine*—apparently, his record company deal was about as close to contract slavery as was legally allowable. Needing money—and an outlet for how pissed off he was—Reznor went out on the first Lollapalooza tour. Of course, he couldn't play all his parts live by himself, so he began hiring sidemen to help out on tour (the most notable of these was guitarist Richard Patrick, who would go on to front one of the '90s' best alt-metal groups, Filter). With dark and damaged imagery to match the music, Nine Inch Nails then proceeded to blow audiences away. Reznor established himself as a musician and performer worth watching.

Although NIN's first record was synth driven, it didn't take long for Reznor to realize that guitars had to be an essential part of the aggression he wanted to unleash. He next recorded the *Broken* EP, a thinly disguised attack on TVT that established him as more than a one-album wonder. From the first moment of the EP, it was clear that the guitar had become Reznor's sound device of choice. On "Wish," the EP's signature tune, the guitar was so distorted and overdriven that it was barely recognizable as a 6-stringed instrument. But it was "Last" that proved to be NIN's guitar tour de force. With savage and relentless metal riffing, Reznor absorbed the metal genre into his own twisted world by distorting the sounds of the guitars into something never heard before—and rarely since.

Broken's appeal prompted Interscope Records to get involved in funding Reznor's second full-length album, *The Downward Spiral*, which he recorded in his studio at home (which is the house where Sharon Tate was killed by the Manson Family in 1969). Released in 1994, *The Downward Spiral* turned out to be one of the biggest releases of the year. Although Reznor backed off the angry guitar overdrive of *Broken*, he went in other directions with the instrument. Notably, he brought in Adrian Belew to add radical guitar squonking and noise to the record. Belew was a unique choice to complement Reznor's noise fury given Adrian's own experimental guitar work—particularly the array of elephant sounds and otherworldly guitar voices that he created on his own records and with King Crimson. Belew's most conspicuous contribution to the record is the closing riff to "Mr. Self Destruct," in which the guitars are actually looped back in a repeating pattern for nearly 45 seconds throughout the song's closing.

The success of *The Downward Spiral* took a huge toll on Reznor, who had become a reluctant musical icon and revered metal innovator. He experienced writer's block, fell out with numerous band members and protégés, and spent his time dabbling in soundtracks and other people's projects. When he did re-emerge, five years after *The Downward Spiral*, it was with the sprawling double CD, *The Fragile*. The album debuted at No. 1, but its girth was hard for listeners to swallow. While he had been away, much of the metal world had caught up with him, and metal bands like Marilyn Manson and Filter (both of whom had been the benefi-ciaries of Reznor's musical input) had taken over the charts.

Trent Reznor became as recognizable for his look as for his sound.

In 2002 Reznor put out a live album, *And All That Could Have Been*, reminding everyone how impressive his back catalog was. It was also a testament to the fact that Reznor had been perhaps the single most important solo artist—in any genre—of the 1990s. His pioneering approach to metal guitar—playing it, recording it, and making it relevant in the context of songs—has yet to be duplicated.

GEAR & SETUP

Reznor's guitars are pretty standard stuff: beyond the Parker Fly (he likes the sound of its piezo pickups), he primarily plays a Les Paul Custom, a Gibson Explorer, and a Fender Precision Bass.

He tags on a variety of effects, including classic 1970s stompboxes such as the Electro-Harmonix Big Muff π distortion, Musitronics Mu-Tron envelope follower, Foxx Tone Machine fuzzbox, DigiTech Whammy pedal, Fender Blender, Roland Chorus Echo, and an MXR Blue Box octaver. Reznor augments these with an array of digital and computer-based effects, including the Mutronics Mutator, Eventide Harmonizer, Line 6 Amp Farm modeler, DigiTech 2120 multi-effects unit, and a Zoom speaker simulator. Most of this runs through Marshall heads, but not out of the speaker cabinet. Instead, Reznor plugs the signal right into the board or directly into his Macintosh interface. On his most notable recordings, the guitar sound was abused and reshaped within Studiovision sequencing software and Digidesign's Pro Tools and TurboSynth.

Reznor generally records guitars separately from other instruments. He then sonically alters them and drops them into the mix. In some instances, they are sampled and loaded into the memory of a keyboard, so the guitar sounds are actually triggered with a synth.

Reznor uses a less-adorned setup onstage, primarily because his equipment is in serious danger of getting destroyed during a show. Instead, he limits himself to a Les Paul and an ESP that run through a Line 6 Pod and then straight into the house system.

STYLE & TECHNIQUE

Simply put, there is no style and technique to how Reznor plays. It would be trite to say he breaks all the rules; rather, there are no rules when he plays. Anything—absolutely anything—goes.

A pianist by training, Reznor freely admits that his guitar work, and ability, was minimal until the *Broken* EP. This helps explain his extremely experimental approach to the way the guitar is played and recorded—he isn't constrained by the way the guitar is *supposed* to be played or is *supposed* to be set up. It helps that the playing is primitive and his chord structures are simple, because it's not what is played that matters with NIN, but how it sounds.

An essential element of NIN's sound is that guitars and amps have already melted down when they are recorded. Getting the sound to the breaking point is too easy—Reznor wants the sounds that emerge after they've reached the breaking point, be it speaker damage, amp overload, frazzled pickups, etc.

To that end, there is an endless number of ways to address and employ his technique. The easiest way is to load a heavily effected or distorted pattern or riff into a computer—then beat the shit out of it with editing software. Change the time signature; alter the attack, decay, sustain, and release; cut it into individual bars and then reconfigure them out of order—anything to get something new and unheard of. Proceed to layer each of the finished tracks one on top of the other until the sound is thick and brutal. New layers and overdubs of guitars can be gated and slightly pitch-bent to create a sound that is completely different from the other guitars that have already permeated a track.

Reznor also pushes guitars way up into the mix to the point where the volume meters are quite likely deep in the red zone. So not only does anything go, but whatever is done should be done to the extreme.

LESSON

Examples 13 and 14 are a lesson in stacking parts for tone and effect, much as Trent Reznor does in the laboratory of a recording studio. Begin with Ex. 13, which features a power chord slid around on the 4th and 3rd strings. The tone should be narrow and nasal, and its delivery machinistic. Apply compression if you have it, and come to a dead stop at the end of the repeated phrase.

SELECTED DISCOGRAPHY: NINE INCH NAILS

Pretty Hate Machine (TVT)
Broken EP (Nothing/Interscope)
Fixed EP (Interscope)
The Downward Spiral (Nothing/Interscope)
The Fragile (Nothing/Interscope)
And All That Could Have Been Live
    (Nothing)

RECOMMENDED CUTS

"Wish" (*Broken*)
"Last" (*Broken*)
"Mr. Self Destruct" (*The Downward Spiral*)
"Heresy" (*The Downward Spiral*)
"March of the Pigs" (*The Downward Spiral*)

Ex. 13: Nine Inch Nails

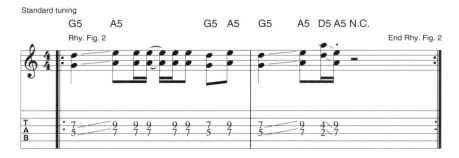

A part like Ex. 13 might be cut-and-pasted into various sections of a NIN song. But to endow it with any power, you'll need to heap additional, similar recordings on top of it in the studio (or get a bunch of guys in the same room playing the same part with the same guitars and amps). Here is the riff again (Ex. 14), but this time some bass and midrange have been added to a copy of the part. Plus, the riff has been recorded again an octave lower. Oh, yeah—and the lower part was doubled and that double EQ'd for more low end. All of this, though, from the same guitar with the same pickups selected.

Ex. 14: Nine Inch Nails

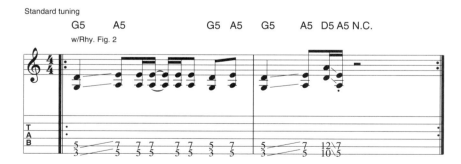

The uptempo Ex. 15 finds Reznor more in the mood of speed punk. Power chords (root-5-root) hover around the 7th fret, moving upward and back in chromatic steps. The same riff repeats twice before a quick chromatic ascent on adjacent strings; the fact that it's out of key and somewhat unexpected contributes to the sense that it's been cut and pasted. However, it's all delivered live.

Two guitars were recorded for this example: one ratty, raspy version with the mids sucked out, and one with very little treble and a fuzz distortion. Each is panned about 90% to one side, so balance your speakers right or left to hear the contrasting tones. The full effect, though, is best appreciated by boosting your stereo's volume to "Stun" and sticking your face dead center between the speakers.

Ex. 15: Nine Inch Nails

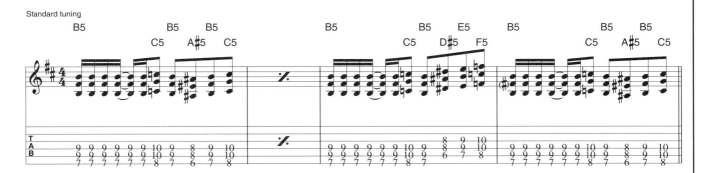

CHAPTER 5
Helmet

PAGE HAMILTON

Helmet was and is the vision of Page Hamilton, perhaps the most eclectic metal guitarist on the planet. From his start as an aspiring jazz player to his involvement with the pre-eminent guitar symphony of its time to frontman for Helmet, Hamilton has played more styles of music than most guitarists will ever hear. In the process, he helped define the sound of new metal, honing the art of stop/start rhythms with atomic-clock precision and incorporating levels of political and social anger into a sound that was thicker than cast iron in concrete.

BIOGRAPHY

Page Hamilton was born May 8, 1960, in Portland, Oregon. The first band he took a liking to was Led Zeppelin—*Led Zeppelin IV* inspired him to buy a guitar and learn the album's songs note for note. His love of Zeppelin led him to rock bands like Pink Floyd, AC/DC, and Aerosmith. Those were his musical inspirations—until he heard the straight-ahead jazz of George Benson. Impressed by Benson's delicate playing and phrasing, he investigated jazz styles and jazz players. He immersed himself in the genre, developing a taste for many jazz instrumentalists, from guitarist Wes Montgomery to saxophonist John Coltrane.

He decided to pursue the jazz side of his musical interest, heading to New York to attend the Manhattan School of Music as a graduate student. After finishing with a master's degree, he threw himself in the avant-garde music movement in New York. There he met Glenn Branca, the foremost practitioner of classically inspired guitar noise. Branca was a composer who put together large groups of guitarists to play symphonies based on droning overtones, a method that produced phantom tones (and even instrument sounds) from the combined frequencies of variously tuned guitars. Guitarists Thurston Moore and Lee Ranaldo had recently left Branca's orchestra to form Sonic Youth, and Hamilton's knowledge of both jazz and rock made him an apt replacement.

After recording and touring with Branca (often playing a guitar that had all six strings tuned to *E*), Hamilton joined New York avant-rockers Band of Susans. The band used the same kinds of droning guitars as Branca, the minor difference being that they applied those drones to actual songs. Hamilton was featured on BOS's *Love Agenda*, released in 1988, but he left shortly after that album, wanting to write his own songs and front his own band. The result was Helmet, formed in 1989. It included drummer John Stanier, bassist Henry Bogdan, and guitarist Peter Mengede—all of whom were enlisted to help Hamilton create a heavy yet disciplined sound.

The band's sharp-as-razors music quickly separated it from the randomness of grunge bands and sloppier metal, and garnered it a deal with indie label Amphetamine Reptile. Helmet released its first album, *Strap It On*, in 1990. Though raw, skilled, and ferocious, Helmet's brand of metal was summarily lumped in with grunge, and the band ended up on tour with Nirvana. The band's live intensity attracted major-label interest, and in 1991 Helmet signed to Interscope. The next year it released *Meantime*, heralded as the new direction of metal. Hamilton's delivery of riffs timed to the split second coupled with bootcamp-abuse vocals endeared Helmet to those who wanted something more meaty and commanding than grunge. "In the Meantime" and the radio hit "Unsung" became anthems for the newest generation of headbangers.

The band misstepped with *Meantime*'s follow-up, 1994's *Betty*. Hamilton had decided to turn away from what was expected and went almost anti-metal. He also replaced Mengede with guitarist Rob Echeverria. More musically indulgent, as well as more melodic and intricate, *Betty* was soft on the ground-pounding guitars and shouting. On the other hand, it was heavy on the experimental and complex, and featured various alternate tunings that gave the record a lighter feel. Unfortunately, fans avoided it in droves.

Even Hamilton realized that he had gone too far in a new direction for his audience. After *Betty*, Echeverria left to join Biohazard, and Hamilton decided to handle all the guitar parts himself. The result was 1997's *Aftertaste*, an album that combined the best elements of the two previous records. Songs like "Diet Aftertaste" and "Birth Defect" displayed the swollen and crushing riffs of *Meantime*, while

Another Page: Hamilton onstage in his pj's.

demonstrating more of the sonic versatility and interesting lead playing he had revealed in his occasional session work (such as his tasteful contributions to Joe Henry's *Trampoline*). But after going so far afield with *Betty*, Hamilton had a hard time bringing fans back with *Aftertaste*.

Helmet toured in support of the record (with Chris Traynor handling the rhythm parts), but Hamilton's brand of skilled and efficient metal was already getting supplanted by nu-metal bands like Korn that wrote catchier, accessible metal and were more attuned to teenage angst than he was. Dismayed, Hamilton pulled Helmet's plug in 1998. He then went to work as a sideman and producer for a number of other acts, including time spent as the temporary replacement for Wes Borland in Limp Bizkit and touring with David Bowie as Reeves Gabrels' replacement.

In 2003 Hamilton said he was reforming Helmet with an entirely new lineup. The band did not yet have a label, and Hamilton told Billboard.com that he got annoyed every time he saw a signed new metal band "playing a riff I wrote 10 years ago." If that comment came from anyone other than Page Hamilton (or Justin Broadrick), it would sound like sour grapes. In Hamilton's case, it happens to be the truth. His influence, if not his name, is evident in almost every band who has entered the new metal arena. Interscope released *Unsung: The Best of Helmet* in January 2004. The label also re-signed Hamilton, who has promised to make a new record. When he does, guitarists will get another chance to hear the sound and playing that helped define new metal.

GEAR & SETUP

Hamilton's gear is almost as eclectic as his background. You won't find any other metal guitarists using the same combination of equipment, or even the same mix of manufacturers. The ESP Horizon Custom is his main guitar, outfitted with Di-Marzio pickups and heavy D'Addario strings. He also uses a G&L SE-2, a Classic ASAT, and several Paul Reed Smith models. He uses Clayton picks.

Hamilton admits that he changes his rig regularly. For much of the Helmet material, he plugged into a Harry Kolbe preamp which went into a Marshall 2204S 50-watt head, then into a Mesa/Boogie SimulClass 2.90 amp. Those powered four Kolbe cabinets. He also used VHT amps, and some of Helmet's earliest recordings featured a Yamaha GEP-50 effects processor set to "Heavy Metal."

For effects he relied on vintage MXR boxes, an Eventide H3000, a Moog Phaser, Z-Vex Fuzz Factory, Frostwave Resonator filter, Lexicon MPX G2 processor, and Rocktron switchers.

STYLE & TECHNIQUE

The linchpin to Hamilton's style in Helmet is rhythm. Essentially, he uses the guitar as a percussion instrument. His strumming and his movement of chords complement and counter individual drum beats—the two instruments move in martial lockstep. In Helmet, timing is everything.

The surgical precision of Hamilton's style cannot be overemphasized. His stop/start strumming—so distinctive and unique in the early '90s that he should have patented it—cuts the guitar off without any sustain and starts it up again with maximum attack. This means serious right-hand control over everything from which strings are strummed to damping and muting. It is not a continuous right-hand movement like that used by Metallica, which resembles a buzzsaw. Rather, Hamilton's style is more like flipping a light switch on and off at high speed. It helps to think of his guitar sound as almost pure attack with no time allowed for decay.

When creating a riff, his approach is completely antithetical to that of someone like, say, Tool's Adam Jones. Hamilton believes in finding a good strong riff idea and building an entire song on that. Thus, the riff is repeated throughout the tune, often continuously (an approach taken by Linkin Park, Mudvayne, and Godsmack). By adding dynamic elements—a change in tone, layering, etc.—the repetition also creates tension, which is what gives Helmet's music much of its anthemic quality.

Less distinctive than his rhythm playing, his soloing is cut from the same cloth as that of many hard rockers. It does reveal the droning noise influence of Glenn Branca, where lead lines are used as noisy interruptions to the verse and chorus rather than precise musical statements. He will occasionally employ shred-like phrasing to his leads ("He Feels Bad" from *Meantime*), but it is all but obscured under the heavy rhythms, squalling feedback, and effects built up around it.

LESSON

A distinguishing characteristic of Helmet is the stark contrast of loud guitars and complete silence. If you were to recreate such parts in the recording studio, you might consider muting between every chord stroke; better, though, to be careful with your guitar technique. For good measure, use a noise gate set to close fast so there's no amp hum between chords.

It's all eighth-note rhythms for the chords played in Ex. 16 (see following page), but with some subtle twists and unexpected changes of direction. Dropped-*D* tuning allows for straight barre chords until the 3rds are added on the 3rd string.

SELECTED DISCOGRAPHY: HELMET

Strap It On (Amphetamine Reptile)
Meantime (Interscope)
Born Annoying EP (Amphetamine Reptile)
Betty (Interscope)
Aftertaste (Interscope)

RECOMMENDED CUTS

"Better" (*Meantime*)
"Turned Out" (*Meantime*)
"Unsung" (*Meantime*)
"Pure" (*Aftertaste*)
"Diet Aftertaste" (*Aftertaste*)
"Driving Nowhere" (*Aftertaste*)
"Birth Defect" (*Aftertaste*)

Ex. 16: Helmet

Track 16

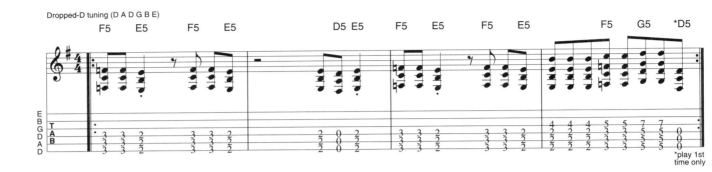

A tight riff in *D* minor lays down a bottom-heavy groove on the 6th string in Ex. 17. Use palm muting to add tension, releasing only about half their pressure at the end of the riff.

Ex. 17: Helmet

Track 17

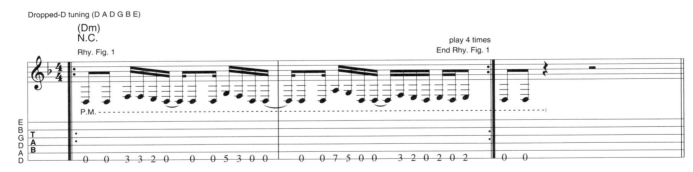

With the previous example providing rhythm, a noisy lead cuts across the top. For a schooled and disciplined player, Hamilton can sound like he's careering out of control, though inevitably his parts resume composure and prove it was all well planned.

The lead in Ex. 18 is played loosely against the rhythm, beginning with strums on open strings and on harmonics before going into a "properly" picked lead. Slow it all down and take away the razor-sharp distortion, and you actually have a nice blues part. *Note: Rhythm part pans left, lead pans right.*

Ex. 18: Helmet

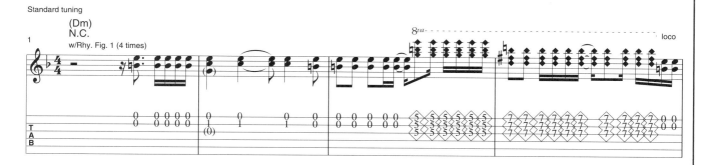

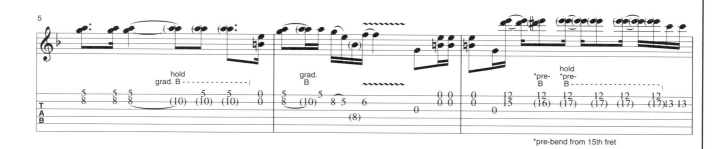

CHAPTER 6
Korn · Limp Bizkit

HEAD AND MUNKY OF KORN

Korn can rightfully lay claim to starting the "nu-metal" movement and all that that entails, good and bad. Drawing heavily from the cold and droning riffs of Godflesh, the stutter-step rhythms of Helmet, and the funk of Faith No More, Korn brought pummeling metal to the masses in an accessible form. The key to its success was taking the guitar sludge of grindcore and speeding it up, adding lyrics that could be understood—and related to on a teenage level—and adding just enough of a hook to make radio programmers take notice. Since the style's rise to prominence in the mid 1990s, many nu-metal bands have cited Korn as a major influence—or have copied it to the point of parody. The band's use of the 7-string guitar (in place of drastic 6th-string detuning) made lower frequencies part and parcel of all new metal bands and forced guitarists to rethink just how low their guitars could go.

BIOGRAPHY

Brian "Head" Welch (born June 16, 1970, in Torrance, California) met James "Munky" Shaffer (born June 6, 1970, in Rosedale, California) in high school. As a child Shaffer had snipped off the tip of his left-hand index finger in the chain of a three-wheeler, and he picked up the guitar as part of his rehab. He spent much of his time listening to Aerosmith, Faith No More, and offshoot Mr. Bungle.

By the late 1980s, Shaffer had formed a band called LAPD (Love and Peace Dude), with Reginald "Fieldy" Arvizu on bass and David Silveria on drums. Welch, a fan of AC/DC, Queen, and Mötley Crüe who jammed with Shaffer, was a volunteer roadie and sometime second guitarist. Playing what they referred to as "heavy punk," LAPD eventually left Bakersfield for the bright lights of Los Angeles. The band released several EPs and one LP, *Who's Laughing Now*, between 1989 and 1991.

LA didn't treat LAPD very well, and in 1993 the band tossed its vocalist overboard and broke up. Re-forming with Welch on guitar, they moved to Huntington Beach and performed as Creep. On a trip home to Bakersfield, Welch and Shaffer heard local band SexArt, which was fronted by lead singer and sometime coroner's assistant Jonathan Davis. They asked Davis to join Creep, and within a month they were calling themselves Korn. The name was the subject of much scrutiny, and there were claims that it stood for everything from Kern County Morgue (where Davis worked) to an acronym for "kiddie porn."

Davis, who admitted to having serious psychological issues ever since working in the autopsy lab, introduced dark and twisted lyrics to the band's sound. In addition to heavy rock, that sound now incorporated the funk that Shaffer had picked up from listening to Faith No More. It was the perfect kind of angst for metal kids who had had it up to their eyeballs listening to whiny grunge kids since the early 1990s.

Davis's themes of alienation, sexual confusion, anger, and betrayal—all taken from the Heavy Metal 101 handbook—meshed well with the metallic sound that Shaffer and Welch had developed. In order to make their sound heavier than other SoCal metal bands, the two adopted the 7-string Ibanez Universe guitars popularized by Steve Vai. First Shaffer, then Welch took on the huge instruments, using the 7th-string *B* to add a rattling bass thrum to their sound. Welch allegedly developed his habit of playing slouched over the guitar because he couldn't get his hand around the neck of the 7-string while standing up straight.

In 1994 the band was signed to Immortal/Epic and released its debut, simply titled *Korn*. The album's songs were considered too dark and damaged for radio and MTV, but the band's constant touring in California landed them opening spots for some of their metal forefathers, including Ozzy Osbourne and Megadeth. Over the course of two years, with virtually no airplay, *Korn* sold 700,000 copies and Epic was ready to release a follow-up. The result was *Life Is Peachy*, which contained the band's first radio hit, "A.D.I.D.A.S." (All Day I Dream About Sex). The album earned Korn a headlining gig at Lollapalooza, but Shaffer contracted viral meningitis and the band decided to drop out rather than perform without him. After his recovery the band put together the first "Family Values Tour" with emerging new metal bands à la Ozzfest.

1999 saw the release of the band's biggest album, *Follow the Leader*. The single "Freak on a Leash" not only got Korn huge amounts of airplay, but it won video awards at both the MTV Video Music Awards and the Grammys. *Follow the Leader*

The crouch rock of Korn (l–r): Head, Fieldy, Jonathan Davis, and Munky.

and 2000's *Issues* both debuted at No. 1 on the Billboard charts, cementing Korn's status as leaders of the new metal movement. *Issues* was perhaps the band's most industrial-sounding record, incorporating grinding guitar work with trancelike drones and enough funk to make it the perfect soundtrack for a mosh pit. During the Issues tour, drummer Silveria injured his wrist and was replaced by Faith No More's Mike Bordin—a fitting example of the band's influences coming around full circle.

Korn followed with *Untouchables* in 2002 and *Take a Look in the Mirror* in 2003. The band's sound varied only slightly from record to record, the changes driven mostly by what was ailing Davis at any particular moment.

Korn's influence on modern metal cannot be overstated. The band got Limp Bizkit its first major-label deal and was responsible for getting fellow Californians the Deftones national exposure. Davis's half-brother, Mark Chavez, is the vocalist for Adema, a band that found itself in a major-label bidding war without having ever played a live show—all because Chavez was related by blood to Korn. And while much of its dark, disturbing, and detuned music can be traced directly to its inspirations, no band integrated those elements for public consumption as well as Korn.

GEAR & SETUP

For Korn, the purpose of all their gear is to make sure they get the lowest sound they can possibly get. There are three elements in achieving this sound: the use of Ibanez 7-string guitars, a mixture of different amps and cabinets, and the way the cabinets are miked.

First come the guitars. Shaffer uses an Ibanez K-7 with the astrological symbol for Cancer inlaid at the 12th fret. He had a Hipshot Trem-Setter added to keep it in tune and to stabilize the floating bridge. He uses nickel-steel medium-gauge Dean Markley strings, .011–.060. Welch plays an Ibanez custom shop K-7 with an ebony fretboard (the standard model comes with rosewood). He also uses Dean Markley strings, although they are lighter gauge at the high end, .010–.060.

In the studio, some overdubs have been tracked with a 1964 Fender Telecaster for variation. Interestingly, neither guitarist has embraced the Ibanez K-14 yet—a 14-string version of the K-7 developed especially for them—claiming it's a little hard to finger.

The Kornboys tend to play the same amps and effects as each other due to a long-term friendly competition over gear (which apparently stems in part from Welch selling Shaffer his first guitar, at a steep markup). The studio setup for the most recent record included a Mesa/Boogie Road King, Triple Rectifier, and rackmount Dual Rectifier, and a Peavey Wiggy. The Mesas, in particular, are chosen for their ability to handle the extremely low frequencies and rumbling generated by the 7th string—and the detuning—of Korn's guitars. (The need to handle these low frequencies adequately holds true for most new metal bands.) All the amps run simultaneously through a Mesa/Boogie 4-channel switcher, and are all hooked up to Marshall cabinets except for the rackmount Rectifier, which goes direct to the board.

The guitarists are effects junkies, claiming to have dozens if not hundreds of effects at their disposal. The Digitech XP100 Whammy Wah is the staple, along with Dunlop Univibe; Electro-Harmonix Big Muff π distortion, Small Stone phaser, and Electric Mistress flanger; Boss chorus and delay; and a Prescription Electronics Depth Charge. Many of their effects pedals end up on their concert pedalboards in order to replicate the sounds from each album.

For their concert setup, the band tends to travel with what they used on the most recent studio record, so the rigs change from tour to tour. Welch and Shaffer typically use a Diezel VH4 for dirty tones, in addition to the Mesa Road King. When using the Road King they both use the dirtiest setting, which is all tubes on.

STYLE & TECHNIQUE

Though they often use the same equipment, the Korn duo usually do not play the same parts. Shaffer develops the riff and tonal feel, while Welch works on melodies to complement the riffs. They write together in the studio and then record independently. Welch is always on the left, Shaffer on the right, and both are hard panned. This has been true of all their albums except the first one, in which the sides were reversed.

The band used to use standard tuning, even on the 7-string—*BEADGBE* (low to high). But as other new metal bands adopted the 7-string, notably Limp Bizkit, they dropped down a whole-step to get an even deeper rumble than their musical competitors. The current tuning is *ADGCFAD* (low to high). On the most recent record, they capoed several songs at the first fret.

Occasionally, they will use an alternate tuning in which the *G*-string is brought back to normal pitch while the others remain down a half-step. That makes the tuning *ADGCGAD* (low to high).

Given the standardization of the guitar choices, it comes down to the amps and the miking that make the Korn sound unique. The band experiments with a dozen cabinets prior to recording, narrowing their selection down to the four they like best for the sound they want for the album. Once the cabs are chosen, they are set out on the studio floor and miked with up to five mics each. The amps are played at ferocious volume, and the sound is mixed using the various mic feeds. The last several albums have been recorded directly to a Euphonics R1 digital hard-disk system.

SELECTED DISCOGRAPHY: KORN

(All on Immortal/Epic)
Korn
Life Is Peachy
Follow the Leader
Issues
Untouchables
Take a Look in the Mirror

RECOMMENDED CUTS

"Blind" (*Korn*)
"Make Me Bad" (*Issues*)
"Falling Away from Me" (*Issues*)
"A.D.I.D.A.S." (*Life Is Peachy*)
"Freak on a Leash" (*Follow the Leader*)
"Got the Life" (*Follow the Leader*)

WES BORLAND OF LIMP BIZKIT

Limp Bizkit was little more than Fred Durst's hobby when he met Korn in 1995. After a show in Florida, several members of Korn stopped in at the tattoo parlor where Durst worked. After tattooing them, Durst struck up a friendship with the band. Eventually, he worked up the nerve to pass on his demo tape, which featured Wes Borland on guitar, Sam Rivers on bass, and John Otto on drums. Korn liked the mix of rap and rock and decided to help Durst out. They arranged for Limp Bizkit to tour with House of Pain and Deftones (another group of Korn friends), and also hooked the band up with their record producer and management company. When House of Pain broke up, Pain's DJ Lethal became the fifth member of Limp Bizkit, and the band put together its first album, 1997's *Three Dollar Bill Y'All*.

The breakout of LB's debut was nothing short of astounding, led in large part by Durst's ability to get the media to report on everything he said and everyone he allegedly dated. Over the course of three records—*Three Dollar Bill Y'All, Significant Other*, and *Chocolate Starfish and the Hot Dog Flavored Water*, as well as "Take a Look Around," their update of the *Mission: Impossible* theme—the band came out of nowhere to dominate the rock airwaves in the late 1990s, competing primarily with Korn and other nu-metal bands like Staind, Disturbed, and Papa Roach.

The heavy rumble of LB's sound—the part that offset Durst's white-boy belligerent screeching—was delivered by Borland's 7-string Ibanez. Borland, who had played the guitar since he was 12 and joined the band when he was 18, was the antithesis of Durst. He was artistic and flamboyant, which often put him at odds with Durst's fratboy style. Borland was a quirky presence during the band's live show, painting his face white and wearing long black robes and black contact lenses to create an eerie onstage persona.

LB's success allowed Borland the freedom to release a solo album in 2001 under the name Big Dumb Face. Unfortunately, the record was an admitted bad joke that failed horribly. Equal parts Gwar and Primus, the album was more Saturday morning cartoon than metal excursion, and it left a sour taste in a lot of people's mouths—Borland's included.

Borland dropped out of Limp Bizkit in late 2001, claiming that he was bored and didn't want to go through the motions with the world's most popular rock band just for the money. His attempts to form a new band called Eat the Day, however, ended in failure when he claimed in late 2003 that he couldn't find a vocalist he liked. That same year, Bizkit finally replaced Borland with former Snot guitarist Mike Smith, who came on just in time for LB's fourth album, *Results May Vary*.

Nu-metal's toxic avenger, Wes Borland.

Heavily influenced by the sound of his mentors in Korn, Borland used the Ibanez Universe 7-string for LB's first two albums. (He claims this choice was primarily due to Ibanez giving him a free 7-string.) Interestingly, he replaced the low-*B* 7th string with a high *E*, then offset this by tuning down a step and half, which resulted in a tuning of *C#F#BEG#C#C#* (low to high). Even though he dropped the low *B*, literally, he still dropped the tuning low enough to create that Korn-like bass growl.

SELECTED DISCOGRAPHY: LIMP BIZKIT

(all on Interscope)

Three Dollar Bill Y'All

Significant Other

Chocolate Starfish and the Hot Dog Flavored Water

Results May Vary

RECOMMENDED CUTS

"Nookie" (*Significant Other*)

"Take a Look Around" (*Chocolate Starfish and the Hot Dog Flavored Water*)

"Rollin'" (*Chocolate Starfish and the Hot Dog Flavored Water*)

He also created an Ibanez 4-string hybrid, using a standard 6-string and replacing the low *E* with an .085-gauge bass-guitar *A* string. Then he added the normal *A*, *D*, and *G* strings, and tuned the whole thing down to *F#F#BE* (low to high).

For *Chocolate Starfish*, he switched to a Paul Reed Smith 6-string—joking he could afford to buy a new guitar that wasn't a 7-string freebie—along with a group of more traditional guitars, including a Gretsch hollowbody and a Fender Jazzmaster.

Like the Kornboys, Borland favors Mesa/Boogie Dual and Triple Rectifier amps as well as Diezels, some of the only amps able to handle the frequencies delivered by his various Ibanez guitars. He runs these through Mesa FX12 cabinets. He uses a surprising array of vintage and unusual effects, including an Ibanez flanger, a Maestro Echoplex, an Electro-Harmonix Q-Tron envelope follower, and an EBow sustainer.

Borland admits that much of his playing on LB records is just hammering away at the guitar to get a sound or a rhythm, and there isn't a lot of finesse involved. Although he has cited Les Claypool and other bass players as influences, little of that style has been evident on record outside of a shared appreciation for funk. Part of his decision to give up the 7-string was a concerted effort to go back to learning the fundamentals of the 6-string.

LESSON

No 7-string? No problem. Get close by tuning down a whole-step (to *DGCFAD*). If you have a Whammy pedal, get down another step by setting it to "Drop Tune" (which processes all input one step lower). That puts you two steps below standard, where you can perform Guitar 1's part in Ex. 19. Notice how short the second note of the riff is, and how the third note is anticipated—if you played it straight, the part would lack momentum.

Guitar 2 is simple and clean, but in conjunction with Guitar 1 it comes across as downright eerie. Throughout the part, stay in position with your 3rd finger planted on *F#*, adding the octave *D* punches around it. Use a chorus with the rate and depth settings full on.

Track 19

Ex. 19: Korn

Gtr. 1 tuned down 2 whole-steps, one w/whammy pedal (C F Bb Eb G C)

Gtr. 2 tuned down 1 whole-step (D G C F A D)

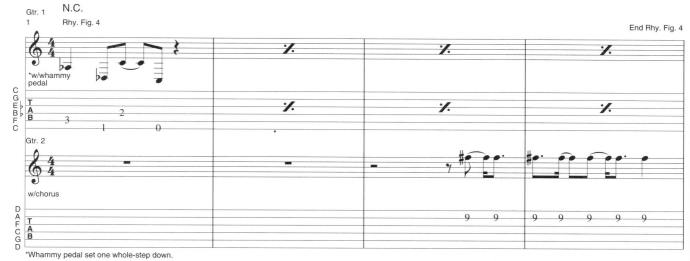

*Whammy pedal set one whole-step down.

Here's another way of slicing the clean/dirty combination. Metal bands are smart to set up this kind of disparity because contrasting parts lend perspective to one another. When one part sounds small and squeaky-clean on its own, the other can sound enormous and filthy.

Both guitars in Ex. 20 are tuned down a full step. Guitar 1 plays a meek arpeggio on just the 3rd and 1st strings. A little bit of flanging and an almost complete removal of lower frequencies (by dialing them out with an EQ) leave this part trembling in the corner. Guitar 2 comes in like a nightmare, its low-string harmonies almost lost in the distortion. The second chord especially, with its $A\flat$ and $E\flat$ clashing with the open D, sounds less like a guitar than something ugly with its jaws open.

Ex. 20: Korn

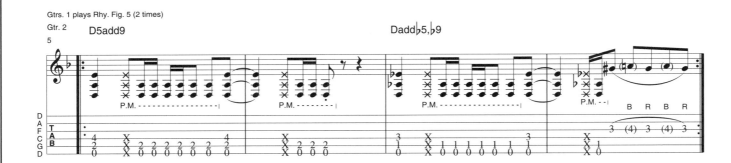

Even if you don't take the step of swapping out your low *E* for a bass-gauge string, as Borland has done, you can get his woolly sound with a majorly overdriven rectifier and most any guitar tuned down 1½ steps. (Guitars with taut action usually fare better.)

Note that even in the wash of overdrive, the percussive thump of palm-muted notes cuts through Ex. 21's pattern of 16ths. The technique and tone go a long way toward establishing the Limp Bizkit's big bottom end—in other words, more junk in the Bizkit trunk.

Ex. 21: Limp Bizkit

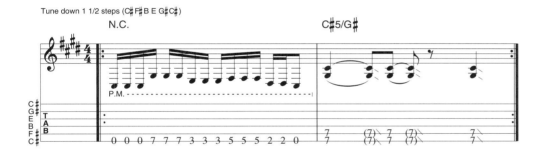

The first half of Ex. 22 mimics a bass part rather than a guitar part, but it helps reveal the band's sense for funk rhythm figures. Sounds pretty cool on guitar, too. The part gets its Primus-y feel from the oddball harmony and the timing of the double-stop figures played up in XII position. The same double-stop shapes are mirrored on adjacent strings after you punch overdrive.

Articulate the first double-stop pair with upstrokes. The addition of the minor-2nd *E♭* into the low *D* (bars 6 and 8) makes the part that much more sinister. Minor 2nds are always good for that.

Ex. 22: Limp Bizkit

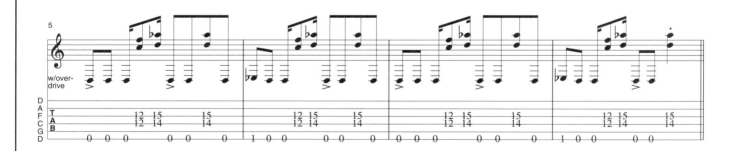

CHAPTER 7
Linkin Park

BRAD DELSON AND MIKE SHINODA

For a band that has released only two studio albums, Linkin Park has managed to become the millennium's reigning king of the nu-metal world. The group has deftly woven together metal, rap, techno, and pop to create the most radio-friendly—and the best-selling—incarnation of nu-metal to date.

Hidden beneath its slick veneer is an aggressive and unrelenting guitar attack that props Linkin Park's sound up on pilings of dense metal. Elements of Helmet's machinistic rhythms and NIN's software-tortured layers are key components of Linkin Park's brand of nu-metal. Propelled by guitarists Brad Delson and Mike Shinoda, Linkin Park's heaviness is almost a stealth element of the band's otherwise polished presentation.

BIOGRAPHY

Linkin Park began as a gathering of high school friends laying down tracks. Guitarist Brad Delson (born December 1, 1977, in Agoura, California), vocalist/guitarist Mike Shinoda, and drummer Rob Bourdon recorded tracks in Shinoda's bedroom studio. Delson, who had been playing since he was in the sixth grade, was a fan of heavy rock like Guns N' Roses, Metallica, and Skid Row, while Shinoda had taken his inspiration from more urban-sounding bands like Anthrax and Public Enemy.

After graduation, Shinoda went to Pasadena's Art Center College, where he met DJ Joseph Hahn, while Bourdon met bassist Darren "Phoenix" Farrell at UCLA. Calling themselves Xero and later Hybrid Theory, the band developed a hip-hop rock style led by Delson's heavy grooves (influenced by Metallica and Skid Row) and

Brad Delson, a very pretty PRS, and some nice headphones.

Shinoda's emcee-style rapping. After working with a vocalist who ultimately didn't work out, they found their final member in Chester Bennington, an Arizona native who had grown up on bombastic classic rock like Foreigner. His vocal style was big and over the top—the ideal metal complement to Shinoda's machine-gun vocals. In 1999 the six-piece band, now known as Linkin Park (Bennington's suggestion and intentional misspelling based on a park he lived near), started playing up and down the Sunset Strip—the area of Hollywood that had once been the proving ground of heavy metal and big hair bands a decade before.

Linkin Park had a penchant for developing heavy guitar riffs that lent themselves to the style of both its vocalists—perfect for Judas Priest–style screeching

Mike Shinoda and a mod-art Ibanez RG.

and RATM-style rapping. For all the elements in the band's mix, its guitar sound, supplied primarily by Delson, was always front and center, delivering crunching power chords, melodic and catchy riffs, and even single-note accents. Unlike other bands who mixed such diverse styles together—usually dropping the guitar to spotlight the vocals or mixing it under the electronics—Linkin Park never lost sight of the metal appeal of their concoctions.

After establishing themselves as a fixture at LA's legendary Whisky A Go-Go, the band was signed to Warner Bros. in late 1999. Within a year, Linkin Park released *Hybrid Theory* and headed out to support the record. They toured with P.O.D., Deftones, Papa Roach, and other nu-metal bands, while *Hybrid Theory* crept up the charts. In 2001 the album reached No. 1 and stayed there for months. Eventually it sold more than 8 million copies, making it the best-selling nu metal album ever, and one of the music industry's biggest rock-band debuts.

Taking advantage of the digital recording equipment they always carried on the road, Linkin Park reworked old songs and in 2002 released *Reanimation*, a remixed version of *Hybrid Theory*. The band was still riding high in 2003 when it released its second studio record, *Meteora*. The disc showed that the success of Linkin Park's first album had not been a fluke—it debuted at No. 1. The most polished songs were the ones embraced by radio, but it was Delson's sledgehammer guitar on cuts like "Don't Stay" and "Hit the Floor" that showed Linkin Park's true metal core. His thick, steroidal tone was as pugnacious as anything laid down by contemporaries like Korn, Limp Bizkit, or P.O.D..

In 2004 Linkin Park was back on the road promoting the record, part of a seemingly nonstop tour that began with the release of *Hybrid Theory*. This time, however, the group took out P.O.D. as their opener—a sure sign that things had changed in the nu-metal world.

Linkin Park is one of the few groups of the millennium to exhibit any staying power. It owes a huge amount of this to its ability to integrate so many diverse styles into one accessible sound. Its best guitar work is not the material that ends up on radio, a condition many metal bands past and present have had to contend with (Queensryche and Alice in Chains come to mind). Listeners expecting to hear radio-friendly cuts end to end will be stunned upon encountering some seriously bonecrushing tones and riffs from the band. Because of this, Linkin Park has found the perfect middle ground as nu-metallists for every season.

GEAR & SETUP

Brad Delson gets his tone from the kinds of equipment popular with many new metallers. He uses PRS Custom 24 guitars strung with D'Addario strings (10XL). He also uses an Ibanez 7-string on two songs, "Run Away" and "With You." He has also played an Ibanez RG7620 and Ibanez Artwood acoustics. His amps are Mesa/Boogie Dual Rectifiers, which he uses with Mesa cabinets (usually in a one-head/two-cabinet configuration). His sound is relatively straightforward, although he does use some pedal effects, primarily from Boss, including a compression sustainer, chorus, and digital delay.

He tunes down a half-step, except for the 6th string, which is tuned down a step and a half (*C#G#C#F#A#D#*, low to high); that's dropped-*D* half a step lower.

Mike Shinoda is known primarily as the band's emcee, yet he is responsible for writing and playing some of Linkin Park's guitar parts. His basic setup—PRS guitars and Mesa Boogie amps—mirrors Delson's, and he too has played Ibanez RG's.

Interestingly, the band's songs and sound are overwhelmingly digital creations. A digital studio is built into the band's tour bus, where it records everything straight to computers (much of Linkin Park's writing takes place while the band is on the road). Parts are written, recorded, cut, copied, pasted, and edited on Mac G4s running Digidesign's Pro Tools. Everything except vocals can be done with this setup, using software plug-ins that mimic amps and provide effects, such as Line 6's Amp Farm.

The songs and parts are documented in Pro Tools as soon as the band writes them, and all the parts are kept for potential use in a final mix.

SELECTED DISCOGRAPHY: LINKIN PARK

(All on Warner Bros)
Hybrid Theory
Reanimation
Meteora

RECOMMENDED CUTS
"One Step Closer" (*Hybrid Theory*)
"Crawling" (*Hybrid Theory*)
"Lying from You" (*Meteora*)
"Don't Stay" (*Meteora*)
"Hit the Floor" (*Meteora*)

STYLE & TECHNIQUE

Delson's style is about delivering a blast-furnace intensity to complement Bennington's enraged vocals, and then pulling back to let Shinoda's rapping come through. It's as if he has two styles for two different bands—which is part of Linkin Park's appeal. Chords are usually loud and ringing, pulling as much sustain as Delson can get from his PRS guitars. He will also stutter his strum and mute the strings during transitions (such as on "Lying from You"), creating a scratching sound that is usually synced with the drums.

Delson's big, in-your-face riffs are multi-tracked in order to give them a runaway-diesel-truck growl that rises above the rest of the band. Riffs often run through the entire song (notably on "Don't Stay"), providing an underlying foundation that allows the vocalists and other instruments to ramble over the top.

LESSON

Half the battle in metal guitar is achieving a properly frightening tone. The motor-breath roar of Ex. 23's LP part results from a number of factors, so don't kick yourself if you can't get the same tone out of your archtop and Fender Champ.

First, the guitar is tuned to dropped-*D* down a half-step (and since the whole riff is on the 6th string, you can just tune your low *E* down to *C#*). A DigiTech Whammy pedal, almost ubiquitous among metalheads, is also a big help. If you have one, set it to add a 5th above the pitch you finger. If not, it's easy enough to add the 5th manually by barring straight across the 6th and 5th strings (don't forget to detune)—but the tone will not be as tight and throaty as it is on our recording. Finally, it's important to know that when you hear a heavy guitar on a recording, you're usually hearing *several* guitars, or a single recording that is copied and then manipulated several times over.

Case in point: the example looks innocent enough, but actually represents four guitars. One guitar was recorded through a Whammy pedal, which added a 5th; then that part was copied, with the second version getting a boost of bottom-end EQ. Cheating? Yeah. But you don't want to be the one who doesn't know the tricks.

Ex. 23: Linkin Park

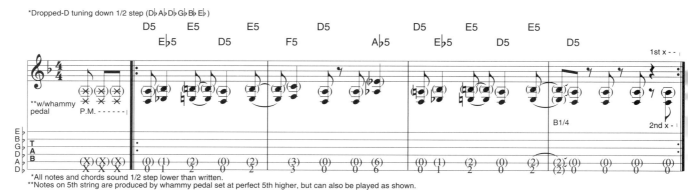

*Dropped-D tuning down 1/2 step (Db Ab Db Gb Bb Eb)

*All notes and chords sound 1/2 step lower than written.
**Notes on 5th string are produced by whammy pedal set at perfect 5th higher, but can also be played as shown.

Chords built on stacked 5ths resonate strongly on an overdriven guitar and add a nice harmonic color; in a world of power chords, the unexpected appearance of a 9th can be a breath of fresh air. (Note: The 9th is heard because the chord is built by starting with a root, adding a 5th, and then adding the 5th above that. The second "5th" is actually the 9th scale degree above the root.) Example 24 features a progression based on such chords, broken up with an octave fill.

Ex. 24: Linkin Park

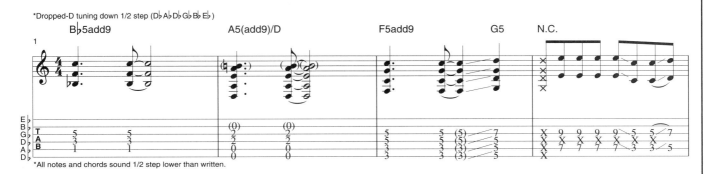

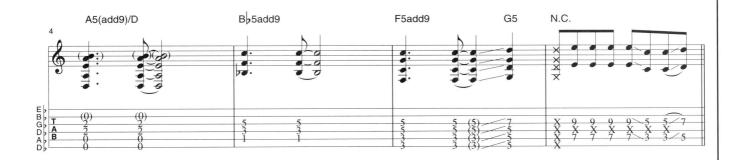

This snappy little dance of death is an open-position riff (Ex. 25). Strike the strings hard with your pick to get a popping and somewhat tortured sound. Once you get the rhythmic feel together, the notes that fall off to open strings will drop naturally into place.

Ex. 25: Linkin Park

ON THE CD

Track 1: Ex. 1, Tool

Track 2: Ex. 2, Tool

Track 3: Ex. 3, Tool

Track 4: Ex. 4, A Perfect Circle

Track 5: Ex. 5, Rage Against The Machine

Track 6: Ex. 6, Audioslave

Track 7: Ex. 7, Audioslave

Track 8: Ex. 8, P.O.D.

Track 9: Ex. 9, P.O.D.

Track 10: Ex. 10, Godflesh

Track 11: Ex. 11, Godflesh

Track 12: Ex. 12, Carcass

Track 13: Ex. 13, Nine Inch Nails

Track 14: Ex. 14, Nine Inch Nails

Track 15: Ex. 15, Nine Inch Nails

Track 16: Ex. 16, Helmet

Track 17: Ex. 17, Helmet

Track 18: Ex. 18, Helmet

Track 19: Ex. 19, Korn

Track 20: Ex. 20, Korn

Track 21: Ex. 21, Limp Bizkit

Track 22: Ex. 22, Limp Bizkit

Track 23: Ex. 23, Linkin Park

Track 24: Ex. 24, Linkin Park

Track 25: Ex. 25, Linkin Park

Track 26: Tuning

All tracks performed by Rich Maloof and recorded at OopStudios in Brooklyn, New York.

ACKNOWLEDGMENTS

The authors wish to acknowledge the following for their help in creating this book:

Thanks to editor Richard Johnston and publisher Matt Kelsey at Backbeat Books for the opportunity to develop The Way They Play into a full-fledged series. Our continued appreciation to the rest of the Backbeat team as well, especially Nancy Tabor, Amy Miller, and Nina Lesowitz. Additional thanks to Jesse Gress for transcribing the lessons. This book follows *The Blues-Rock Masters* and *The Acoustic-Rock Masters*, and with any luck will lead us to many more masters in the years to come. Our thanks also extend to Philip Chapnick, who encouraged us to find a home for The Way They Play within his publishing group.

Thanks to Paul Muniz of the DigiTech/Harman Music Group for providing the Whammy pedal.

Thanks as always to Pete Prown, partner in many things—including crime—whose insights, critiques, and constant browbeating always result in something that much more interesting. His books *Gear Secrets of the Guitar Legends* (with Lisa Sharken; Backbeat Books) and *Legends of Rock Guitar* (Hal Leonard) are must-reads for any guitarist.

HP Newquist would like to thank:

Thanks first and foremost to Rich Maloof, who found himself immersed deeper in metal than he ever imagined. His uncanny ability to distill the musical and tonal essence of bands as diverse as Godflesh, Tool, and Audioslave has made this book as enjoyable to play as it is to read. If not for Rich's diligence, friendship, and ability to carry on lucid conversations after 2 AM, this book would never have seen the light of day.

Thanks to Trini, Madeline, and Katherine, the women who make it all worthwhile. Not only do they have to listen to the sounds of my skull-crushing music as it rattles the walls of the house—now they can read about it, too.

Finally, thanks to those individuals who indirectly played a part in the creation of this book. To Tony Iommi, whose influence and hospitality I have been meaning to acknowledge for many years. Crediting him here is long overdue, and hopefully puts it all right. To Al Mowrer, who has shared my passion for distorted and decibel-driven guitars for more than two decades. To my brothers, sisters, and parents for being as supportive and indulgent as any musician in a big family has a right to expect. To everyone else who taught me how to write a better sentence or figure out a complex chord progression. Thanks, one and all.

Rich Maloof would like to thank:

My biggest thanks to Harvey Newquist, the brains behind The Way They Play. If you think living in the 'burbs and raising beautiful kids makes one soft around the edges, Harvey can set you straight. His suggestion to make every music example in this book as outsized, assertive, and genuine as possible mirrors his worldview. For that, and for years of unwavering friendship, he has my appreciation.

Thanks to the friends of mine who didn't get old when everyone else did, especially John Donato and Erik Wolf.

My one-year-old son bobbed his head in rhythm to the Godflesh riffs. I see a mosh pit in his future. And my wife might not be stagediving at the next SOAD show, but she knows a good riff when she hears one. Like everything I do, this book is for Kris and Daniel.

PHOTO CREDITS

Jay Blakesberg: pages 39 & 69

© Kevin Estrada / Retna Ltd.: page 31

Ken Settle: pages 12, 25 & 57

© Ian Tilton / Retna UK: page 43

©Y´Brengola / All Action / Retna Ltd.: page 29

Neil Zlozower: page 49

ABOUT THE AUTHORS

HP Newquist and his writing have appeared in publications as diverse as *The New York Times*, *Rolling Stone*, *USA Today*, *Variety*, *Billboard*, and *Newsweek*. He has written a dozen books, including *Music & Technology* (Billboard Books), *The Yahoo! Ultimate Reference Guide to the Web* (HarperCollins), *The Brain Makers* (Macmillan), and *Legends of Rock Guitar* (with Pete Prown, published by Hal Leonard). His magazine articles have covered topics from musicians and medicine to artificial intelligence and virtual reality. His film credits include writing the Emmy-nominated music documentary *Going Home* for the Disney Channel. Based in Fairfield, Connecticut, Newquist is former editor-in-chief of *Guitar* magazine. He has been playing guitar since he was 15 years old, which seems like a very long time ago.

Rich Maloof is an independent editor and writer based in Brooklyn, New York. He has written dozens of instructional pieces for musicians, including two previous volumes in Backbeat Books' The Way They Play series (with HP Newquist) and *The Alternate Tuning Reference Guide* (Cherry Lane). In 2003 Maloof authored *Jim Marshall: The Father of Loud* (Backbeat Books) and founded *InTune*, a classroom magazine for music students.

Maloof served as editor-in-chief of *Guitar* magazine until 1998, when he launched his own business. Among his clients to date are Berklee Press, *Billboard*, CNN, TrueFire, and Yahoo! He has been playing guitar for over 25 years, and really should be better by now.

see it.
hear it.
nail it.

www.TrueFire.com

H.E.A.R.
hearnet.com™

Photo by Chauky Davis

"The real reason that I haven't performed live for a long time is that I have very severe hearing damage. It's manifested itself as tinnitus, ringing in the ears at the frequencies that I play the guitar. It hurts, it's painful and it's frustrating."

-H.E.A.R. Founding Donor,
Musician Pete Townshend
Rolling Stone Magazine July, 1989.

H.E.A.R. is HERE for musicians, DJs, sound engineers, music fans and anyone that may need help with their hearing.

"H.E.A.R. is how you can HELP"

Visit our website for hearing resources. Make a contribution online, or donate your tax deductible items for the H.E.A.R. Charity Auction on Ebay.

Contact:
PO Box 460847
San Francisco, CA 94146
415-773-9590
hear@hearnet.com
WWW.HEARNET.COM

© H.E.A.R. 2003

H.E.A.R. is a non-profit 501(c)(3) organization

WHEN IT COMES TO GUITARS, WE WROTE THE BOOK.

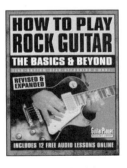